THE EMPLOYMENT OF AFRICAN AMERICANS IN LAW ENFORCEMENT,

1803-1865

THE EMPLOYMENT OF AFRICAN AMERICANS IN LAW ENFORCEMENT, 1803-1865

LIEVIN KAMBAMBA MBOMA

Published by Lievin K. Mboma Press

ISBN: 978-0-9989716-3-6 (hardcover)
978-0-9989716-4-3 (paperback)
978-0-9989716-5-0 (ebook)

Manufactured in the United States of America
LCCN 2017919367

Cover image: Library of Congress. Nov. 1865. "Guard House and Guard, 107th U.S. Colored Infantry Fort Corcoran near Washington, D.C." Other title "Arlington, Va., Nov. 1865. 107th U.S. Colored Infantry, Guard and guard house shown, Fort Corcoran." Library of Congress Web site. Jpeg. http://www.loc.gov/pictures/item/2013648641/ (accessed March 14, 2018).

CONTENTS

ACKNOWLEDGMENTS   ix

PREFACE   xiii

INTRODUCTION   xv

CHAPTER I   1
Entrance of African Americans into Law Enforcement during the 1800's in the South
African American Militiamen before the Civil War
     in Tennessee and Mississippi Territory
The Employment of African Americans in Law
     Enforcement in Louisiana

CHAPTER II   20
Maintenance of Law and Order in the Plantations Before the Civil War
African American Law Enforcement Officers
     at Brierfield and Hurricane Plantations
Police Work
African Americans as Officers of the Plantation Court
African American Jurymen
Jury System in the Brierfield Plantation

Correction
Perception of Walter L. Fleming on African American
    Court Officials
Role of Jefferson Davis in the Administration
    of Punishment
James Pemberton

CHAPTER III   31
**African American Law Enforcers Before the Civil War
in the Northern States**

CHAPTER IV   42
**The Emancipation Proclamation and the Employment
of African Americans in the United States Army**

CHAPTER V   62
**African American Law Enforcement Duties During the
War of Secession**
    Law Enforcement Services Performed by African
        American Soldiers
    Patrol Services
    Emergency Services
    Making Arrests
    Escort Services by Colored Troops
    Guarding Prisoners of War
    Prison Camp Under Colonel Hallowell at Morris Island
    Regulations in the Prison Camp
    Duties of the Guards in the Prison Camp
    Jail Services after the War
    Guarding Government and Private Properties

CHAPTER VI   110
**Law and Order in the Blacks' Civil War
Settlements and Villages**
    The Village of Mitchelville
    School Attendance in Mitchelville

The Little Contraband Village in Chattanooga
The Government of G. Campbell
Black Watchmen in St. Simon's Island

CHAPTER VII   120
**African American Spies, Scouts, and Informants
in the War of Secession**
John Scobell
James Lawson and Black Bob
Harriet Tubman
Robert Smalls

CHAPTER VIII   136
**African American Spies in the Confederate
White House**
Mary Elizabeth Bowser in the Confederate
White House

CHAPTER IX   140
**James H. Jones and Benjamin Montgomery Deeds
for President Jefferson Davis**
Benjamin Montgomery

CHAPTER X   147
The Scouting and Spying of Dabney and George Scott
Dabney, the African American Scout
George Scott

CHAPTER XI   150
Conclusion and Summary

BIBLIOGRAPHY   153

INDEX   159

ABOUT THE AUTHOR   175

ACKNOWLEDGMENTS

A book's ideas may be orchestrated by a single author, but I received support from various people to aid in its completion. From the beginning to the final draft of this book, I received tremendous support and constructive criticism from many professors, archivists, and librarians, including family friends. Similarly, academic editors also provided much guidance and counsel for the feasibility of this book. Without the contributions of the people listed above, I would have had numerous challenges to complete the final draft of this manuscript. With the assistance of professors and academic editors, many obstacles, which would have increased the difficulties of piecing together this book were diminished. Of the professors whom helped to guide my thoughts, I would especially like to note Professors Marvin W. Dulaney, Joel Duck, Kenneth J. Peak, and Adebayo Oyebade. Professor Kenneth Peak of the University of Nevada, Department of Criminal Justice, was very helpful on advising me about the difficulties I would encounter while writing this manuscript and also encouraged me to endure all the difficulties that I would confront during the publishing process. Professor Pippa Halloway, director of African Studies at Middle Tennessee State University, read the first two drafts of the manuscript and provided valuable ideas as well as guidance on how to put together a feasible book. Professor Marvin W. Dulaney, the chairperson of the Department of History at the University of Arlington in Texas, offered me many documents for my research. When I was in Texas, he provided me with an office, as well as transported me from the school to the hotel where I resided at the time of the visit. I am grateful for his academic and material support. Professor Joel Dark, associate dean and history professor at Tennessee State University in Nashville, has spent time counseling me and reviewing the manuscript from the first draft. His office was always open to me when I needed his counsel. Moreover, Professor Oyebade, Chair Person of the Department of History at Tennessee State University in Nashville, was devoted to my writing cause. He spent time advising and provided encouragment to me during my research journey. Similar to Professor Dark, I was always welcomed in his office when I needed academic assistance.

As other scholars, I acknowledge the input of Professor Jewell Parham at Tennessee State University. As an English Instructor, scholar, and editor, she made worthy contributions to this work. She had a binding tie with the topic under examination because of her passion for African and African American history and literature. For these reasons, she was devoted to the success of this work. In addition to providing guidance and engaging in stimulating conversation, she edited a few chapters of this book.

Similarly, I credit Miss Ramona Shelton, history instructor at Motlow State Community College. She copyedited and reviewed the final draft of the manuscript and her contributions are worth noting. In addition to Miss Ramona, I credit Dr. Antoinette G. Van Zelm for asking pertinent questions relevant to the text. Due to her contributions, I was able to modify the time-frame of my research. Similar to academic agents, Stephanie S. Rodriguez, manager, and Megan Sheridan, librarian, assisted me consistently with technical support at the Southeast Public Library. Thank you also to future American history scholar Rossell Brewer for reading a chapter of the book and offering editorial suggestions.

With respect to archivists, Dr. Tom Kanon provided me with vivid support, such as the analysis of data collected for the completion of the manuscript. He also read the first draft of the manuscript, providing salient suggestions and constructive criticism. Similarly, he shared with me his writing experience for his own book. In addition to Dr. Kanon, Miss Kelley Sirko, Program Coordinator at the Metro Nashville Archive and John Lodl of the Rutherford County Archives were very helpful in giving healthy comments for the improvement of the manuscript. In South Carolina, I received support from Miss Marianne Cawley who sent me various data regarding law enforcement duties performed by black soldiers during the war of secession, including the fall of Charleston.

In Tennessee, I am grateful to have had the help of Vanderbilt University, Fisk University, Tennessee State University, Tennessee State Archives, and Davidson County Archives librarians for providing the authoritative documents for my research. As for other institutions of knowledge, I am grateful for the support I received from the Edmondson Pike Librarians.

Among the editors, Mr. Craig Gill, editor at the University of Mississippi Press, devoted his time and energy into reading the entire first draft of the document. He also shared the document with his colleagues, thoroughly revised the manuscript, and suggested areas of improvement. Like the editors of the Mississippi Press, Mr. Thomas Wells, Acquisitions Editor at the University of Tennessee Press, revealed the areas of improvement as well. He highlighted the areas of focus so that the book would be interesting and contribute to the academic arena. Dr. Alexander Moore, the Acquisition Editor of the University of South Carolina Press, was open to discuss with me the events of the Civil War as it happened.

Finally, but certainly not least, I appreciate the support which I received from loving family and close friends such as Hajar Khailini, Robert Pullen, Armando Mpembele, Jarvis Sheffield, special collections librarian at Tennessee State University, and Ernest Miah. I also acknowledge Keata Brewer and Charles Sutherland at E. T. Lowe Publishing for guiding me through the production process from final manuscript to printed book.

PREFACE

The study of the employment of blacks in law enforcement has not been thoroughly investigated. There are few documents relating to the inclusion of African Americans in law enforcement. Scholars from various fields of study, such as history, law enforcement, police science, and political science have investigated the entrance of African Americans into America's body politics, but the chronological study of this ethnic group in American law enforcement is less explored. On the contrary, there is plenty of literature on the enrollment of free African Americans into the militia of Louisiana. Similarly, there are abundant studies on African Americans' contributions in the Civil War and other wars.

Contrary to the studies examined by many scholars on the employment of African Americans in law enforcement, this current study chronologically relates the events which led to their inclusion in law enforcement in the order in which it actually happened during the period under the exploration. This study initiates the exploration of the entrance of African Americans into law enforcement (the militia) since the earlier years of American's administrations in Louisiana. After this period, their enrollment in the War of 1812-1814 is also investigated. Moreover, military law enforcement duties performed by African Americans during the execution of the Civil War is examined in this book.

This study is not a response to all the questions which will arise about how African Americans were involved in law enforcement in local and state governments throughout the United States. But it discusses the circumstances which led to their inclusion in law enforce-

xiv | AFRICAN AMERICANS IN LAW ENFORCEMENT, 1803-1865

ment before the Civil War as well as during the execution of the war. The circumstances which I discuss had direct impact on the behavior of American policy makers. To illustrate, the pressure of the wars in 19th century United States shaped the behavior of some state and federal government officials and the way they perceived free African Americans in issues regarding the security and safety of the Territory and the State of Louisiana. Government officials such as General Andrew Jackson of Tennessee, during the 1812-1814 war, stressed to African Americans that the United States needed them to fight for her security.[1] The perception of General Jackson indicates that the pressure of the said war impacted his decision to enlist African Americans in the militia of some southern states for the cause of the United States. As during the Civil War, Union generals employed African Americans as military law enforcement officers.[2] Likely, they were assigned to spying and intelligence collection during the Civil War.[3]

Notes

1 Arsene Lacarriere Latour, *Historical Memoir of the War in West Florida and Louisiana in 1814-1815.* John Conrad and Company, J. Maxwell Printer, 1816.

2 In the Civil War Archives, Union Regimental Histories of the United States Colored Troops, data showed that 12th Regiment Infantry organized in Tennessee on July 24 to August 14, 1863 was assigned to guard duties for the defense of the railroad in Nashville. This infantry was stationed at the department of Cumberland.

3 Allen Pinkerton, *The Spy of the Rebellion: Being a True History of the Spy System of the United States Army during the Late Rebellion. Reveling many Secrets of the War Witherto not Made Public.* University of Nenraska Press, 1883.

INTRODUCTION

The entrance of Africans Americans into law enforcement in the United States was not an easy task. People of color faced many obstacles before their inclusion into the enforcement of the law. In the colonial era, they were from time to time employed as militiamen in their respective colonies, but they were excluded from performing civilian law enforcement duties in the South. With respect to civilian law enforcement during the colonial era, Wentworth Cheswell, an African American, was appointed justice of the peace in Newmarket, New Hampshire. He continued to serve in law enforcement even during the early American republic.[1] Contrary to the North, it was in 1800 that African Americans were authorized to perform civilian law enforcement duties controlling runaway slaves. This was the case in Louisiana where they were part of the state's militia during the reign of the French and Spanish.[2]

Even though African Americans were employed in law enforcement before the Civil War, their entrance into maintaining law and order has been overlooked. There are many discrepancies with respect to the matter in question. There are few longitudinal research studies explaining the entrance of people of African descent into law enforcement. Professor Marvin W. Dulaney has reconstructed the involvement of African Americans in law enforcement in the United States since the Louisiana Purchase.[3] He revealed salient information on the employment of African Americans in law enforcement during the war of the rebellion. Unlike the work of Professor Dulaney, this current research reveals vivid information regarding African American law enforcement duties before the Civil War in the North and the South and during the Civil War. While Professor Dulaney's book is concerned with black police in the United States, this present work explores the involvement of African Americans in various law enforcement duties such as police work, judiciary, and regulatory assignments. In addition, prison duties performed by African Americans during the Civil War are also documented.

With respect to the employment of African Americans in law enforcement in the South, I discuss Louisiana before the Civil War and during the War of 1812. I also explore the contributions made by African Americans of other states, such as Tennessee and Mississippi, for the security and safety of the South before the war of the rebellion. In addition, I also discuss the War of 1812 as well as the Battle of New Orleans in 1814. In regard to African Americans' law enforcement duties, I reveal pertinent information about Wentworth Cheswell and various black officers such as John Mercer Langston and Allen Maccon.[4]

As in Louisiana and in the North, various law enforcement duties were performed by African American soldiers during the Civil War. During this period, they performed patrol, emergency, and guard services. Additionally, they had the power to make arrests, control and deter crimes. Moreover, they were protecting civilians in the areas under their jurisdiction. Furthermore, I discuss the correctional duties performed by African American soldiers in the prison camps as well as in the federal prisons in various cities.

African Americans were employed as law enforcement officers in the United States before the Civil War in limited numbers. Data indicates that in the South and North, African Americans held law enforcement positions. In the South, they served as militiamen. In the North, they were appointed as minor judiciary officers. During the Civil War, African American infantries were vested with the power to make arrests, detain, and escort prisoners of war. Likely, they were tasked with guarding prisoners of war. They were also entrusted with police work in the areas under the occupation of the Union. But in towns and villages where they were disliked, African American infantrymen were prohibited from conducting police duties.

Notes

1 James Hill Fitts, *History of Newfield, New Hampshire*. The Rumford Press, 1912.

2 Francois-Xavier Martin, *The History of Louisiana*. Printed by Lyman and Beards Lee, 1827.

3 Marvin W. Dulaney, *Black Police in America*. University Press of Indiana, 1996.

4 John Mercer Langston, *From the Virginia Plantation to the National Capitol*. American Publishing Company, 1894. For the account of Allen Maccon, see W. Irwin; American Agent, A Tribute for the negro. Harned, new York, 1848, p.141.

CHAPTER I

Entrance of African Americans into
Law Enforcement during the 1800's in the South

The employment of African Americans into law enforcement was not done overnight in the United States. There were many obstacles that prevented black men from being accepted into this arena. First, African Americans were not fully considered as citizens in the majority of states in America. Although the Constitution of the United States protects the citizenship of every person born in the land, this protection was not extended to African Americans. In fact, due to their slavery status, there was a time when the black man was counted only as three-fifths a person. Therefore, it is no wonder that they were always excluded from government employment such as law enforcement, particularly for being hired as policemen. Throughout the southern states, there were many free people of color, but they were not part of the American body politic. No data has been found indicating that free blacks were employed in the municipal government as it relates to the police work, except in Louisiana. It appears that they were legally excluded by law from entering law enforcement at this level. However, in some states free African Americans were permitted to enroll in the militia. For example, in Tennessee and Louisiana, African Americans were part of the militia of the states before the 1815 skirmishes began between Great Britain and America.

African American Militiamen before the Civil War in
Tennessee and Mississippi Territory

In the state of Tennessee, free African Americans were enlisted in the militia and defended the territory as did their white brethren. During the War of 1812, black men were prominent among those who protected lives and properties in the Mississippi Territory. Tennessee historians, Professor Bobby Lovett at Tennessee State University and Tennessee State archivist and historian, Tom Kanon, have recorded in their academic work that free African Americans enjoyed the privilege of serving in the militia the same as other Americans.[1] These writers have also listed a few names of free African Americans who served in the War of 1812. According to Professor Lovett, during the military conflict between the Creek and the Americans in 1812, Christopher Christian, Caesar Prince, Robert Renfro, Phillip Thomas, and Jeffrey Locklier were free African American militiamen who served under General Andrew Jackson.[2] While Kanon did not list the names of African Americans enrolled in the Tennessee militia in 1812, he noted that Major Locklier served with General Jackson during this particular war. The account of Major Locklier has been recorded by many American historians for his exceptional courage during enemy attacks. According to Joseph Thomas Wilson, when American soldiers disbanded under the pressure of the enemy, Locklier fearlessly mounted his horse, took command of the battle, and routed the enemy. For his military endeavor, General Andrew Jackson bestowed upon Locklier the well-deserved honor of "Major." Though "Major" was not a legitimate military rank given to Locklier, from thereafter, he was always called Major Locklier. This African American was highly respected in Nashville among people of his color as well as whites who were familiar with his valorous military deeds.[3] In the record of Davidson County, militiamen were listed for taxation purposes.

In 1812, African Americans in the Mississippi Territory were an integral part of the defenders of freedom and liberty. From the account of the Mississippi Historical Society, data shows that African Americans were enlisted in the militia of the Territory in the capacity of waiters, servants, private servants, and privates. It is unknown whether the servants were armed or not. In the same territory, Samuel Smith told a doctor that Captain Dixon Bailey and his brother were with an African American militia who defended with them Fort Mims, a stockade in Alabama. Smith witnessed a large and powerful African American man wielding an axe who killed more Indians than any other defenders in the fort. He died after being wounded by a Native American who cut the Negro with a knife and tomahawk. The African American who fought at Fort Mims alongside Captain Bailey was a slave. Due to his valorous deeds, he was credited by the Americans as follows: "[S]lave as he was, he fought bravely in behalf of the whites and deserves to be remembered along with Captain Dixon Bailey and his brother Daniel Bailey."[4] The name of the African American credited with Captain Bailey and his brother was not mentioned in the Mississippi Historical Society document. Jack Cato, an African American resident of Clark County claimed that he was a drummer during the War of 1812 that lasted until 1815.[5] On the rolls of Mississippi militiamen, African Americans were identified as "Negro" or "nigger." Some black soldiers were listed with one name only. For example, in the battalion of cavalry under the command of Thomas Hinds, Alfred (nigger) was listed as a servant. Similarly, Benjamin (nigger) was recorded as a servant. In the company of Captain Wilkin's rifle, Ben, an African American, was also noted as servant. In the 18th Regiment (1814-1815) of Mississippi Militia under Captain Joseph Vellio, William (Negro) was listed as a waiter.[6]

With respect to the police force, since African Americans were not fully accepted as citizens, why were they employed in New Orleans as police or law enforcement officers? What facilitated their entrance into law enforcement? The answers to these questions require a careful analysis of the circumstances which led to the inclusion of African Americans in law enforcement in the state of Louisiana. There are many circumstances which caused temporary inclusion of African Americans in law enforcement during the early 19th century. These circumstances which caused the enrollment of African Americans in law enforcement were not uniform in the few states where such employment occurred. Furthermore, the political landscape in the states where African Americans were provided with the opportunity to serve on the police force was not strictly antagonistic to educated or uneducated African American free men. This was the case of free African Americans in Louisiana during the 1803-1816 administration of Governor William C.C. Claiborne. As in Louisiana, Governor

Claiborne served also in the same capacity in Mississippi from 1801-1803.[7] Possibly due to his government deeds in Mississippi Territory, he was once again appointed provisional governor in the Island of New Orleasns and the province of Louisiana. On October 2, 1805, he was appointed governor of the territory of Orleans until its admitance to the Union.[8] This governor established amiable relationships with influential free African Americans in New Orleans. At the time when he decided to form a militia battalion of free men of color, he had an honorable conversation with free men of color in that city. The exchange between them was plausible.

The Employment of African Americans in Law Enforcement in Louisiana

The employment of African Americans in law enforcement in Louisiana can be traced to the French and Spanish administrations. From various documents, records show that the French and Spanish government included African Americans in the militias of the colony. As militiamen, they served during the wars and protected the colony against the enemies of the state. Similarly, African American militia men quelled slave disorders. Historian Robinson Reilly (1974) noted that Spanish governors in Louisiana authorized African American militiamen to perform law enforcement duties such as preserving law and order. It appears that free African Americans were given law enforcement privileges to incapacitate slaves from escaping and to prevent slaves from doing harm to their masters. There is no data indicating that they were permitted to arrest other inhabitants of Louisiana who committed a crime. Both Reilly and Governor Claiborne recorded that two large companies of free African Americans were included in the Spanish government. He also noted that their services to that government were credited.[9]

During colonial Louisiana, African Americans were also employed as commanders of the companies of black soldiers. For example, Simon, a free African American, commanded the company of people of his color.[10] Jean-Baptiste Le Moyne de Bienville, father of New Orleans and four-time governor of Louisiana within the years of 1701-1743, had fifty permanent African American military men under his command.[11] In addition, he employed African American guards. In 1827, historian Francois-Xavier Martin recorded that "Bienville had twelve hundred white, and double that number of Indian and black troops."[12]

Free African Americans and mulattos were also employed as slave police patrols militia in Louisiana. Pedro Piernas, a commandant in Louisiana during the Spanish administration, employed sixteen free African and mulatto militiamen to catch runaway slaves. The salary for these sixteen militiamen was seventeen pesos or six reales a day. This company was under the command of Pierre Thomas, a free African American. The account of Thomas was not discussed in the document located at Tulane University. It is unknown why Piernas was given such responsibility. It is unknown as to whether he was an experienced soldier or militiaman. African American militiamen were part of the security apparatus during the reign of the French and Spanish in Louisiana.

During the colonial French and Spanish Louisiana eras, there were no objections to the inclusion of African Americans in the security apparatus. Governor William C.C. Claiborne noted that free African Americans received the first militia training under the Spanish government. He also recorded that they were always called upon to serve the government.[13] As with the Spanish, under the French, Pierre Clement de Laussat gained control of Louisiana during the period of the Louisiana Purchase (1803) and became the first French prefect of the state. The colonial prefect used the corps of free men of color in Louisiana on December 20, 1803, during the ceding of Louisiana to the Americans.[14] The free men of color paraded as did their white counterparts. After the surrender of Louisiana, the militia companies of free African Americans were neglected by the United States government. It appears that during the Spanish and French government, the inhabitants of Louisiana did not oppose the inclusion of free African Americans in the security apparatus. There are no records indicating the objection of the employment of African Americans in the militia during the Louisiana Purchase era. However, Governor Claiborne revealed that the white natives of Louisiana disliked black people. The governor could not ascertain the reasons the whites disliked them.[15] It is unknown whether the English, Spanish, French or all of these groups disliked black people since the colony was inhabited by many groups. Governor Claiborne did not specify which ethnic group was hostile toward Africans and their descendants. Like the whites, African Americans were also antagonistic to the white Americans. Grace Elizabeth King writes "free Negroes and slaves had their prejudices and supersitions to foster disservice against the Americans."[16]

Regarding the existence of African Americans in law enforcement, historian and sociologist W. E. B. Du Bois wrote in *Black Reconstruction in America* that blacks were recruited in the militia force of Louisiana in 1803. Du Bois' account corroborates with the data collected by many writers, but he failed to mention the hostility toward African American militiamen by the native whites. Even though the corps of Free Men of Color existed in 1803, it seems that after the surrender of Louisiana to the United States, African American militiamen did not have the same status as they had under the Spanish and the French authorities. The corps was disbanded and neglected by the newly organized government. As the Corps of Free Men, the militia corps of the Territory of Orleans was poorly organized. Governor Claiborne lamented the condition of the militia to the United States Secretary of War Henry Dearbon. The governor did not believe that the militia corps of the territory was strong and capable enough to resist an enemy attack without the assistance of the black militiamen.[17]

After the transfer of Louisiana from the French to the Americans, social harmony did not exist among the inhabitants of the Territory of Orleans. Grace Elizabeth King wrote that an insurrectionary spirit was still present among the Spanish and French Creole. Even African Americans disliked the European Americans. King also noted that placards were posted on many corners of the streets against the Americans. These signs became of interest to the public who assembled in those areas.[18] Such kinds of activities were troubling to Governor Claiborne. As a result, he was determined to organize the militia for the territory of Orleans.

In 1804, under the temporary administration of Governor Claiborne, the inclusion policy in the militia materialized. However, the governor used caution when employing African Americans in the militia. In his letter to the United States Secretary of War, data shows that the old inhabitants of Louisiana desired the disbanding of corps of free men of color. Even though white people in Louisiana were not in favor of including African Americans in the militia, the governor understood the urgency of reorganizing his military force. In addition, he was aware that the territory was militarily weak. Therefore, including African Americans in the militia was for the best interest of the United States. Moreover, since the territory was under the threat of the Spanish, it would be unwise for Governor Claiborne to alienate free African Americans because he suspected the Spanish planned to instigate Indians to revolt against the Americans. Therefore, he was obligated to reconsider the inclusion of free African Americans in the militia of the territory. Charles Gayarree, historian, attorney, and politician of the time, noted that the militia which existed under the Spanish government was partially employed by Laussat. When Pierre Clement de Laussat was prefect of New Orleans, the militia forces maintained law and order, including controlling the behavior of runaway slaves. It appears Laussat believed in the services performed by free African Americans during former administrations. He did not see the black military as a threat to planters nor to white people, in general.

Historically, law enforcement duties in Louisiana were military-oriented. The militia forces and soldiers were entrusted with law enforcement duties. Claiborne's administration attempted to retain the militia employed for the security of the colony by Laussat, but the military was disorganized. In the beginning of the American administration in Louisiana, Governor Claiborne was incapable of organizing a militia due to the division which existed among the inhabitants of the territory. The Americans, French, Spanish, and the Creole did not have an amiable relationship. Similarly, the native whites in Louisiana did not want to put weapons in the hands of black men. Therefore, Governor Claiborne sought advice from the Secretary of War regarding the formation of militia companies for the protection and defense of Louisiana.

The antagonistic relationship between the French, Spanish, English, Americans, Creole, and free African Americans was not healthy for the existence of the Territory of Louisiana. Spanish and English subjects were hostile to the rule of the Americans. On the other hand, African Americans seemed to be loyal to the Spanish government. As a result, the Americans formed their own militia group in 1804. Possibly, they established their own militia as a measure to secure their lives and properties against any attacks from the Spanish, the French, the English or African Americans. The state of affairs of the territory was troubling to Governor Claiborne; in fact, he feared the division between the inhabitants of Louisiana because the territory did not have a viable militia. In 1804, Claiborne executed his military plan and informed U.S. President James Madison that the city needed a strict police force. In his letter to the president dated July 3, 1804, he stated that the population of Louisiana was formed of various races and as a result, prejudices existed among them. Likely, each ethnic group of people had different interests. Therefore, he feared to form a government under such conditions.[19] It appears that the government was under difficult conditions and the militia needed to be reorganized because in this territory cohabitations between many ethnic groups was difficult to reconcile.

From this period, Governor Claiborne was very concerned about the state of the security of the territory. Consequently, in 1804 he departed from New Orleans on August 20th and visited many counties of the territory to assist personally in organizing the militia. It appears that the existing militia of free African Americans was recognized by General James Wilkinson, senior military officer and statesman, and the Secretary of War, Henry Dearborn. While Claiborne had difficulties in making public the existence of black militia in the territory, Dearborn was alerted to support such action. In Louisiana, the arming of blacks was detested by many white citizens. However, with support from the Secretary of War, Claiborne appointed Michael Fortier and Lewis Kerr as majors for the battalions of free blacks.[20] Enlisting African Americans in the militia was carefully designed. According to a letter written in 1804 to Major Fortier by Secretary of War Dearborn, data indicated the selection of black militiamen was conducted with some skepticism. As stated in the letter, "[T]he views of the government relative to the free blacks in and about New Orleans deemed prudent not to increase the corps but to diminish [it], if it can be done without giving offence."[21] The letter also advised Major Fortier: "You are instructed to muster no free blacks in your battalion who resided without the city or suburbs, and you will for the present avoid enrolling any new recruit, assigning for reason, that such is the order of the governor, and adding that you are not the cause; but you presume, that the battalion is deemed sufficiently numerous, and free men of color not now attached thereto, may hereafter be formed into a separate corps."[22]

During the Battle of New Orleans in 1814, whites and their free black counterparts aged forty-five years and older were engaged in guarding homes and protecting private properties. In like manner, they maintained order in New Orleans and the surrounding towns and posts. Slaves were engaged in building the walls of defense and widening the canals. Moreover, slaves fortified military positions and fought in several battles as did African American freemen. Free women of color nursed the wounded at hospitals.[23] During the Battle of New Orleans, it appears that the prejudice against African Americans performing law enforcement duties was not exhibited by the inhabitants of the city and its neighboring towns. The maintenance of peace and order was valued by both white and black inhabitants of the city. Charles Allegre and Constant Michel were among the free blacks in Lousiiana who served in law enforcement in 1814. These two African Americans served in the Louisiana City Guard in 1814.[24] According to Dulaney, Charles Allegre was a veteran soldier who served in Fortier's battalion of free men of color. This battalion was formed in 1812 by order of the legislature.[25] In 1814, Charles Allegre was a member of the city guard. While Allegre served in the city guard, Jordan Noble, a free black man, served as drummer during the Battle of New Orleans. This African American was born in Georgia and moved to New Orleans in 1811. In the same year, he joined the United States Army. Possibly, he was in one of the regiments of the free blacks. In the Point Coupee Parish, African Americans also enlisted in the militia. Powell A. Casey recorded that Senator Sebastian Hiriart was adjutant of one of the battalions of free men of color during the Battle of New Orleans. African Americans' rebellious behavior in Louisiana was noted by Governor Claiborne to James Madison, the United States Secretary of State on September 29th, 1804. In his letter to the secretary of state, Governor Claiborne noted that respectable inhabitants of New Orleans signed a petition addressing to him the alarm caused by African Americans. It appeared they requested the strengthening of the night patrol due to the danger caused by African Americans.[26]

The content of the letter reveals the concern government officials had with enlisting African Americans in the militia of the territory. On the 18th of April, 1804, by the order of the secretary of war, the battalion of free African Americans was presented with a stand of colors in order to prevent jealousy among the corps of militia.[27] Casey wrote the War Department had approved the employment of free African Americans in February 1804. He posited that the War Department ordered the recruitment of African Americans with previous militia experience under the Spanish regime.

It seems that with the enlistment of militiamen in the territory, the patrol system in Louisiana was re-organized. Henry Rightor, Louisiana historian, notes that the commander of the new militia force was Colonel Bellechasse. It was under his leadership that the militia patrol was performed. In this militia force commanded by Colonel Bellechasse, ten free African American militiamen were included among the twenty-four officers as noted by historians Peter J. Kastor and Francois Weil.[28] As the militia force of Colonel Bellechasse patrolled the areas prone to disorders and turbulent populations, it was critical to enlist free black men in the force. In Louisiana, the areas or districts inhabited by slaves were considered disorderly because the slaves were prone to escape from their masters. Therefore, in such areas, militia patrols were aggressively organized because slaves were considered to be the turbulent population.

The security of the territory was taken into much weight by the governor. He was aware of the contributions made by the free blacks when they assisted the French and Spanish in the preservation of peace and security. He also knew how the free blacks were attached to the Spanish and French government. Therefore, it was not in the best interest of the American government to alienate and exclude free black men from the security apparatus. For these reasons, Governor Clairborne was obligated to communicate with the Secretary of War on the subject of employing black men as an integral part of law enforcement. As a result, the governor informed the Secretary of War about the appointments of Major Michael Fortier and Lewis Kerr as commanders of the militia of the free blacks. The involvement of Henry Dearborn, the Secretary of War, in the inclusion of free blacks in the militia was a strategic political maneuver on the part of the governor to avoid infuriating native whites in Louisiana who disliked arming the free blacks. It is essential to remember that the black militia battalion that existed during the Spanish and French administrations were disbanded by the Americans. The enlistment of blacks in the militia of 1804 was not formed by law but at the request of the governor, General Wilkinson, and the Secretary of War.

In 1805, under the temporary government of the Territory of New Orleans, Etienne de Bore was appointed mayor. Under his administration, the council ordered the formation of a regular police force for the maintenance of law and order. Even though the police force was formed, the city of New Orleans was under the military government. In regard to the police force, Henry Rightor notes that when the police force was formed in 1805, Livandais and E. Jones were appointed special police commissioners.[29] They were entrusted with the inspections of the prisoners and making police regulations.[30] Fortier notes that under the police act, citizens were ordered to enlist in the militia.[31] It appears that this was the first time in the territory that a militia force was formed in the territory of New Orleans under the auspices of the United States. This force was called the gendarmerie. In the gendarmerie, African Americans were also enlisted. The gendarmerie was formed on April 10, 1805, by the approval of Governor Claiborne "for regulating and governing the militia of the Territory of Orleans." Historian Dulaney notes that the gendarmerie was operational from

1805 to 1806.[32] Men enlisted in this force were ordered to perform military services as well.[33] According to Peter J. Kastor and François Weil, the council ordered the recruitment of twenty-five white men or free mulattoes under the command of white officers.[34] The account of Kastor and Weil was similar to that of Rightor. According to Rightor, legislatures allowed the enlistment of mulattoes because white men refused to serve in the police force due to small pay. Therefore, as white men could not be found to perform police duties, mulattoes might be employed but the officers must be white.[35] Even though mulattoes were authorized by law to serve on the police force, Rightor records that a strong prejudice existed to the employment of African Americans as officers in New Orleans. By law, police work was reserved to white males only. The Ordinance Regulating the City Police enacted by Governor William C.C. Claiborne ordered that "a watch shall be organized to consist of free male white inhabitants of the city between seventeen and fifty years of age who have resided here more than thirty days, excepting always people of authority, regular, practicing physicians, and apothecaries, clergy-men, schoolmasters, officers and soldiers of the regular troops, sea-faring people, and such person as the commissaries of the quarters may for good and special reasons judge to be entitled to an exemption."[36]

The employment of free African Americans among the police officers of Louisiana was consequential. Originally, legislatures did not have any plans for including blacks in law enforcement. The refusal of whites to serve as policemen opened the way for the employment of black officers. Unlike in the Spanish reign and the militia of 1804, African Americans in the gendarmerie were mandated to control the behavior and movement of African slaves, especially runaways. The officers of the gendarmerie did not prevent slaves from escaping. As a result, the force was disbanded and another force was established in 1806.

In 1805, at the end of the temporary military government, the gendarmerie was disbanded. In 1806, Governor William C.C. Claiborne established the New Orleans City Guard (Garde de Ville). In the letter to Henry Dearborn, Governor Claiborne communicated clearly that he planned to lodge the city guard in one of the public buildings. The city guard was under the civil government. Rightor writes that the city guard was the city police. In regard to the enlistment of African Americans, Professor Dulaney and other writers agree that black officers were included in the city guard. The officers of the city guard were also empowered with police services of the city. In 1807, as well as 1808, African Americans were still in the militia in Louisiana. Charles Gayarre contends that almost thirty blacks deserted from the militia during this period. In addition to the gendarmerie and the city guard, there was a small force of watchmen for the preservation of peace and order in the city of New Orleans. The second formation of the second city guard force happened in 1809–1910. In the second city guard force, Dulaney noted that Augustus Bolen was among the officers who patrolled for the search of runaway slaves. The second city guard force was formed on January 1, 1809, because the militia of the territory was not effective and poorly armed. Due to the pressure of the war, there is reason to believe that free blacks were enlisted in the second city guard force as articulated by Dulaney. In this year, the prospect of war between Great Britain and the United States increased, and the anxiety about the formation of the militia was capital.

In 1811, when slaves revolted on the St. John the Baptist plantations, free African American militiamen were dispatched to quell said revolt. As noted by Reilly, the involving of free African Americans in suppressing the slave insurrection was approved by Congress. He writes that two companies of African Americans were formed for that cause. According to Casey, in 1811, there was one battalion of free blacks in the city of New Orleans which was commanded by Major Dubourg. Similar to Casey, Dulaney also notes that free blacks were officers who quelled the slave insurrection of 1811. In the same year, data show that a supplementary militia law was passed before the admission of the territory as a state of the Union. The militia law was passed on April 29, 1811. With the passage of the supplementary militia law, free African Americans were enlisted in the force to quell the slave insurrection as well as for the anticipation of the war between England and the United States.

In 1812, the Territory of Louisiana became a state and the legislatures were elected. With the election of legislatures, the enactment of militia laws was no longer the duty of the governor and the council. Militia laws under the states were established by legislatures with the approval of the governor. When the Territory of Louisiana was admitted as a state in the Union, the war between the United States and Great Britain became imminent. The pressure of war was felt through the entire Louisiana Territory. On June 18, 1812, in an inaugural message, Governor Claiborne requested to the legislature the formation of an effective militia force. It appears that with the pressure of war, enlisting blacks in the militia became necessary. When the state constitution adopted by a convention of representatives in 1812 was framed, African Americans were authorized to enlist in the militia. The article C.12, 1812 authorized the formation of the militia corps of free men of color.[37] Michael Fortier wrote that the Constitution authorized only the enlistment of free black tax payers. With this requirement, certain free African Americans were eligible for militia duties under the commands of white officers. Free African Americans were barred from commanding the militia of people of their own color by the Constitution. As ordered by the Constitution, militia companies of free African Americans were formed for the defense of the states as well as the maintenance of peace. Based upon information from the *Louisiana Digest*, the governor authorized the formation of auxiliary troops of free blacks whose duties were the maintenance of good police. According to the governor, the numbers of the black troops were not to exceed eighty men. After their enlistment, free blacks were required to arm themselves with horses and arms. Resident requirements were taken into account before the approved enlistment of free blacks in the troops reserved for the maintenance of peace in the parish of Natchitoches.[38] The order also required that the enlisted militiamen be the sons of owners of some real property with the value of at least one hundred and fifty dollars.[39] It appears that land ownership was for the first time in the United States enforced by law to police applicants. If this act was not enforced to white police applicants, it can be classified as discriminatory. The enlistment of free men of color for police work in Natchitoches was also recorded by John Codman Hurd. In his work titled *The Law of Freedom and Bondage*, he noted that the Act of 1812. C. authorized a militia corps of free men of color commanded by a white person. On the other hand, the Act of 1815. C.24 ordered the formation of police corps of free blacks in Natchitoches.[40]

In regard to the defense of the territory, General Andrew Jackson issued a proclamation requiring African descendants to defend the state of Louisiana against British invasion. General Jackson was the first of the high ranking military officers to make such a decision to enlist African Americans in the militia under the regulation of the United States in 1814. General Jackson, who was himself a slave owner, utilized strategies to convince and empower African Americans to fight in the war under the illusion that they were citizens of the United States and needed to fight for freedom and protect the territorial integrity of the United States. He made African Americans feel like they were equal citizens and obligated to defend the country as their forefathers sacrificed during the Revolutionary War. He also promised to liberate African slaves after the war. Possibly, due to the promise of being freed from slavery if they became a part of the military to defend America from Britain, many slaves felt obligated to enlist in the militia. Contrary to his appeal, General Jackson did not liberate any African slaves after the war. General Jackson's decision to enlist African Americans into the militia was not challenged by any other officers. To materialize his design, he made a proclamation warranting the enlistment of people of color. His proclamation was as follows:

> Through a mistaken policy you have heretofore been deprived of participation in the glorious struggle for national rights in which our country is engaged. This no longer shall exist. As sons of freedom, you are now called upon to defend our inestimable blessing. As Americans your country looks with confidence to her adopted children, for a valorous support, as a faithful return for the advantages enjoyed under her mild and equitable government. As fathers, husbands, and brothers, you are summoned to rally round the standard of the eagle, to defend all which is clear in existence.
>
> Your country, although calling for your exertions, does not wish you to engage in her cause without amply remunerating you for the services rendered. Your intelligent minds are not to be led away by

false representations. Your love of honour would cause you to deprive the man who should attempt to deceive you. In the sincerity of a soldier and the language of truth, I dress you.

To every noble–hearted, generous freeman of colour, volunteering to serve during the present contest with Great Britain, and no longer, there will be paid the same bounty in money and lands, now received by the white soldiers of the United States, Viz. one hundred and twenty–four dollars in money, and one hundred and sixty acres of land. The non–commissioned officers and privates will also be entitled to the same monthly pay and daily rations, and clothes furnished to any American soldier. On enrolling yourselves in companies, the major–general commanding will select officers for your government, from your white fellow citizens. Your non–commanding officers will be appointed from among yourself.

Due to regard will be paid to the feelings of freemen and soldiers. You will not, by being associated with white men in the same corps, be exposed to improper comparisons or unjust sarcasm. As a distinct, independent battalion or regiment, pursuing the path of glory, you will, undivided, receive the applause and gratitude of your countrymen.

To assure you the sincerity of my intentions and my anxiety to engage your invaluable services to our country, I have communicated my wishes to the governor of Louisiana, who is fully informed as to the manner of enrollment, and will give you every necessary information on the subject of this address.[41]

In the South, African Americans were included in the militia and police force in Louisiana. In the state, free Africans were always enlisted in the militia during the French and Spanish government under the colonial power. In 1803, under the American government, they were also included in the militia. According to historical data, free African Americans were first appointed as policemen in Louisiana through the Union. In other states in the South, they were enlisted in the militia before the Civil War. Records indicate that African Americans served in the militia in the War of 1812 and the Battle of New Orleans in 1814. During this war, they acted as scouts and guards.

Notes

1 Tom Kanon, *Tennesseans at War of 1812-1815: Andrew Jackson, the Creek War, and the Battle of New Orleans*. University of Alabama Press, 2014, p.17. In his book, Historian Kanon mentioned Robert Renfro and three unamed free African Americans were included in the Davison County, Tennessee militia during the 1812 War. He also mentioned the name of Major jeffrey Locklier who served in the same war.

2 Bobby L. Lovett, *The African-American History of Nashville, Tennessee, 1780-1930*. Fayetteville, University of Arkansas Press, 1999, p.8.

3 Joseph Thomas Wilson, *The Black Phalanx: A History of the Negro Soldiers of the United States in the Wars of 1775, 1812, 1861-65*. American Publishing Company, 1890, p.50.

4 Henry Sale Halbert and Timothy Harton Ball, *The Creek War of 1813 and 1814*. Danohue & Henneberry, 1895, p.158.

5 Ibid, p.161.

6 See Dunbar Rowland, Rolls of Mississippi Comands in he War of 1812. Publications of Mississippi Historical Society Centenary Series, vol.4. The Society, 1921, pp.164-213.

7 See Dunbar Rowland, Official Letter Books of W.C.C. Claiborne, 1801-1816, vol.1. State Department of Archives and History, 1917, p.iv. Clairborne was appointed governor of the Territory of Mississippi on May 25, 1801 by President Thomas Jefferson. He served in that territory till March 27, 1803 when he was commissioned in Louisiana. In 1803, Claiborne was identified as Governor General and Intendent of the province of louisiana. At this period of time, he wass still under the provisional government.

8 Ibid, p.1.

9 Ibid, p.312.

10 Charles Gayarrw, *History of Louisiana*. W.J. Widdleton, 1867, p.480. Gayarre notes that in one occasion during the war, when the men under the command of Simon flew, he stood his ground and remained with the French officers at the spot the most exposed until the retreat was sounded. He was a very brave man.

11 Roulhac Toledano and Mary Louise Christovich, *New Orleans Architecture: Faubourg Treme and The Bayou Road*. Pelican Publishing, October 1, 2003, p.94.

12 Francois-Xavier Martin, *The History of Louisiana*. Printed by Lyman and Beards Lee, 1827, p.307.

13 See Official Letter Books of W.C.C. Claiborne, 1801-1816, vol.2. State Department of Archives and History, 1917, p.218.

14 Ibid, Reorganization of the Battalion of Free men of color, pp.216-218.

15 Ibid.

16 Grace Elizabeth King, *New Orleans: The Place and the People*. MacMilliam and Company, 1895, p.166.

17 See Official Letter Books of W.C.C. Claiborne 1801-1816, vol.2. State Department of Archives and History, 1917, p.218.

18 King, 1895, pp.165-166.

19 See Letter To James Madison from Governor W.C.C. Claiborne written July 3, 1804 in New Orleans. Official Letter Books of W.C.C. Claiborne, 1801-1817, 1817, p.239.

20 See Letter To Henry Dearborn, New Orleans 9th June, 1804. In the letter, Governor Claiborne states that he appointed two majors to command the Battslion of Free people of color. He listed mr. Fortier, a native of Louisiana and a merchant was one of the major appointed by him. In the letter, he mentioned that Major Fortier was a respectable man in the state. As Major Fortier, Major Lewis Kerr was also a major appointed for the command of Free men of color. Dunbar Rolland, Official Letter Books of W.C.C. Claiborne, 1801-1812, vol.2. State Department of Archives and History, 1917, pp.190-200.

21 See Letter From H. Dearbon to Governor Claiborne written in Washington, February 20, 1804. Dunbar Rowland, Official Letter Books of W.C.C. Claiborne, 1801-1812, vol.2, pp.54-56.

22 Ibid.

23 See Louisiana State Museum Online Exhibits. The Cobildo: Two Century of Louisiana History of New Orleans. The Battle of New Orleans.

24 Marvin W. Dulaney, *Black Police in America*. Indiana University Press, 1996, p.10.

25 On April 29, 1811, the council ordered the formation of battalion of Free men of color. This act was put into force in April, 1812 when the Territory of Louisina was admitted into the Union. Alicee Fortier, Louisiana: Comprising Sketches of Parishes, Towns, Events, Institutions, and Persons, Arranged in Cyclopedic form, vol.2. Century Historical Association, 1914, p.150.

26 See Letter From W.C.C. Claiborne to James Madison of September 20, 1804 written in New Orleans. Official Letter Books of W.C.C. Claiborne, 1801-1816, vol.2, p.337.

27 Ibid, pp.104-105.

28 Peter J. Kastor and Francois Weil, *Empires of the Imagination: The Louisiana Purchase.* University of Virginia Press, 2009, p.125.

29 Henry Rightor, *Standard History of Louisiana.* Lewis Publishing Company, 1900, p.110.

30 Ibid.

31 Fortier, 1814, p.150.

32 Dulaney, 1996, p.9.

33 Ibid.

34 Kastor and Weil, *Empires of Imagination: Transatlantic Histories of the Louisiana Purchase.* University of Virginia Press, 2009, p.225.

35 Rightor, *Standard History of New Orleans, Louisiana.* Lewis Publishing Company, 1900, p.110.

36 See Ordinance regulating the city police. official Letter Books of W C.C. Claiborne, vol.2, 1917, pp.16-19.

37 John Codman Hurd, *The Law of Freedom and Bondage in the United States*, vol.2. Little. Brown, 1862, p.159.

38 Louisiana. Louisiana Supreme Court, The Louisiana Digest, The Free Men of Color, 1841, p.221.

39 Ibid.

40 Hurd, 1862, p.159.

41 See Arsene Lacarriere Latour, *Historical Memoir of the War in West Florida and Louisiana in 1814-1815.* John Conrod and Company, J. Maxwell Printer, 1816, p.xxxi. Latour recorded the full text of General Jackson Proclamation inviting free African Americans to enlist in the militia for the defence of the Territory of Louisiana against the British.

CHAPTER II

Maintenance of Law and Order in the Plantations Before the Civil War

During the colonial era in America, settlers observed the territorial divisions of their main group of forefathers, the Anglo-Saxons. Each territory in America was partitioned into tithings, hundreds, and shires as in England. According to Sir William Blackstone, during the Saxon era, ten families of freeholders formed a tithing. On the other hand, ten tithings made up a hundred, and a limited number of hundreds formed a shire or county.[1] These territories were under the jurisdiction of local officials. The territories mentioned above were government institutions. Along with the aforementioned territories, many plantations and villages were also local law enforcement agencies. The parish system was enforced in some provinces during this era as well. Land was divided into parishes in Virginia, South Carolina, and North Carolina prior to the introduction of counties. Land was separated into boroughs in New York and Pennsylvania, in addition to towns. As for New England colonies, the town system was enforced. The district system was also observed for militia purposes. Law enforcement officers were elected or appointed in each entity in an effort to uphold law and order.

Plantations represented a patriachal government under the jurisdiction of the owner in the Southern states. Family members of all proprietors, servants, and slaves were under the protection of the plantation government. It appears that in each plantation, components of criminal justice were established. Frederick Douglass, an African American slave, abolitionist, author, politician, and civil rights leader recorded pertinent data on the plantation government. As a slave, at a young age he witnessed the administration of the plantation government. From his own recollection, he noted that the plantation was a government. He illustrated thoroughly the plantation of Colonel Edward Lloyd where he was enslaved. According to his memory, the colonel had many plantations. The home plantation was the seat of the government where daily affairs of the twenty farms were transacted. He went on to note that "all disputes among the overseers were settled here [home plantation].[2] Furthermore, he pointed out that "if a slave was convicted of any high misdemeanor, became unmanageable, or evinced a determination to run away, he was brought immediately here [home plantation], severely whipped, put on board the sloop, carried to Baltimore, and sold to Austin Woolfolk."[3] Douglass reveals significant data on the administration of the plantation criminal justice system. From his revelations, it is sound to note that the components of the criminal justice system were instituted in the plantation.

Frederick Douglass believed that the home plantation of Colonel Lloyd was parallel to a county village.[4] The plantations were divided into many slave quarters and inhabited by many people. To illustrate, three to four hundred slaves worked and resided in the home plantation of the colonel. According to Douglass' estimate, about 1,000 slaves worked throughout the plantations of Colonel Lloyd.[5] With such numbers of inhabitants in the colonel's plantations, it is pertinent to identify his institution as a plantation government. This government was governed by the owner and the superintendent.[6] The officials listed above were law enforcement officers in the plantations and in the home government. A similar administration was in force in the plantations of the Davis family. Similarly, in Louisiana, McDonough and Z. Kingsley permitted the self-governing approach to their slaves.[7] Carter G. Woodson, an African American scholar and historian, noted that the African slaves of McDonough of Louisiana and Z. Kingsley in Florida established the plantation government styles administred by people of their own race. He went on to stipulate that they had a court which was under the jurisdiction of an intelligent African slave among them. The court was under the supervision of an African American overseer.[8] The

African slaves of John McDonough were well prepared on the notion of civil liberties.[9]

In regard to African Americans, data does not indicate their entrance as law enforcement officers in Southern towns, counties, and parishes. On the contrary, in the plantation government, evidence shows that the owner or owners of the plantation government sometimes appointed able African slaves to enforce rules. Authors such as Varina Davis, the wife of the Confederate States president, Edward Austin Johnston, and Booker T. Washington documented the employment of African slaves on the Davis family plantations as law enforcers. Similar data were also recorded by Ulrich Bonnell Philipps in 1918. Philipps writes that African slaves self-governed the Brierfield and Hurricane plantations.[10] As there is little data on this subject, the plantation of Jefferson Davis, the President of the Confederate States, and Joe Davis, a general in the Confederate Army, will be explored for the examination of law enforcement duties and titles held by African Americans before the war. President Jefferson Davis owned the plantation of Brierfield and his brother General Joe Davis was the sole owner of the Hurricane plantation in Mississippi.

African American Law Enforcement Officers at Brierfield and Hurricane Plantations

Before the examination of the maintenance of law and order at the Brierfield and Hurricane plantations, a brief history about them must be documented. According to Varina Davis, the wife of Confederate President Jefferson Davis, Brierfield was built from a portion of land given to Jefferson Davis by his brother Joseph E. Davis. The land which his brother gave to him was named "the Brierfield." Davis, the wife of the president says that the track of land was called 'Brierfield' "because of a dence growth of briers which were interlocked over land."[11] In addition to the land, his brother also gave him African slaves left by his father. On the other hand, the Hurricane plantation was established by their brother Joseph E. Davis. The name 'Hurricane' derived from the event which happened when the plantation was built. According to Varina Davis, when Joe Davis began culvating land with his African slaves, a big storm stopped the work they were doing. Davis' nephew, the son of his brother Isaac was killed. Miss Davis went on to note that "Mr. Isaac Davis's leg was broken."[12] The accounts of the president's wife are authoritative, she resided in the plantation and was well informed of the foundation of that institution. She was part of that organization for many years.

In the Brierfield and Hurricane plantations, African Americans were entrusted with the administration of criminal justice. According to historian Walter L. Fleming, at the Brierfield plantation, Jefferson Davis freely empowered his slaves with the management of social order in the plantation. Fleming also noted that under Jefferson Davis, African Americans governed themselves at the Brierfield plantation. When Union soldiers occupied the plantation, African Americans continued to self-govern.[13] The Montgomery family was trained in the notion of community building and self-governing before the establishment of Mount Bayou. In regard to the components of criminal justice, Fleming recorded that the police and court stystems along with the punishment of law breakers was under the jurisdiction of African Americans. President Davis had only the power to pardon offenders. The information recorded by Fleming was also recorded by Varina Davis.

According to the president's wife, Joseph E. Davis was the architect of the self-governing approach in the plantation government. Davis, the brother of the president, believed that "the less the people are governed, the more submissive they will be to control."[14] With this approach he managed his family and his slaves. Mrs. Davis also stipulated that "he instituted trial by jury of their peers, and taught them legal form at holding it. His only share in the jurisdiction was the pardoning power."[15] The account of Mrs. Davis is parallel to the profession of Joseph Davis. By profession, he was a lawyer in Vicksburg. He studied law and practiced the same. He believed in the notion of civil liberties and local control.

Police Work

In the Brierfield plantation government, Walter L. Fleming noted that Jefferson Davis selected African slaves as sheriffs and constables.[16] These Negro officers were empowered with the maintenance of law and order. With the appointment of such officials, the government was under the Saxon system. Therefore, African American sheriffs and constables had the power to detain and arrest suspected criminals. Likely, the investigation of criminal cases as well as the collection of evidence for criminal acts were under the jurisdiction of the sheriffs and constables. During the period under investigation, sheriffs and constables were entrusted with police work in Southern states. The sheriff was the exeutive officer of the county. He had the power to detain and arrest law breakers. On the other hand, the constable maintained law and order. He also had the power to arrest. In plantation governments, police power entrusted to law enforcement officers were not constitutional. Such power derived from the will of plantation owners. Due to the decentralization system observed in the United States, the President of the United States, national and state law makers, including governors of the states did not have the right to interfere with the administration of the plantation government. It appears that planters were very influential in the states where they resided as such law and order in the plantation government were enforced according to the will of owners. The government system established on the plantations were authoritatian, democratic, or an oligarchy. But on the plantations of Jefferson and Joseph Davis, the democratic system of administration was observed. Hurricane plantation was similar to a small town. The plantation had many slave quarters. Three hundred forty-five African slaves worked in that local entity. It is plausible to say that the authoritarian style of government wouldn't be beneficial to Jefferson E. Davis and his brother. Therefore, indirect rule was enforced for economic and security reasons. In regard to economics, Jefferson and Joseph Davis believed African slaves were productive when they worked freely. With respect to security, African slaves were less likely to escape or cause harm to the owners when they were treated fairly. It seems that they responded well to the authority of a person of their own race rather than that of a white overseer.

Historically, the title of 'sheriff' and 'constable' are antiquated. These titles can be traced to the kingdom of England during the Saxons and the Normans eras. While the title 'sheriff' derives from the Saxon, the title 'constable' was introduced to England by the Normans. In addition to the police, the court was also under the control of African Americans. Judges, jurymen, and counselors of the court were people of the African race.

African Americans as Officers of the Plantation Court

The court is an ancient component of criminal justice. From antiquity, court officials have been entrusted with the adjudication of cases as well as the administration of justice. Like in other entities, at the Brierfield plantation, Jefferson Davis selected shrewd and intelligent African Americans as administrators of the plantation court. In 1908, Walter L. Fleming recorded that the presiding judge at the Brierfield plantation was a person of African descent. He heard and settled cases brought before him. During the court proceedings, witnesses were also examined as in the white court.[17] While Fleming did not mention the name of the African American judge in Brierfield, Morris Schaff noted that James Pemberton was the presiding judge of the plantation court in Brierfield.[18] Data on Pemberton will be discussed later in this chapter.

It is sound to stipulate that Pemberton heard cases against people of his own race brought before him by accusers. It is unknown whether or not civil and criminal cases regarding white people were heard in the plantation courts. Possibly, cases between a planter and his African slaves were adjudicated in the plantation court. In addition to the adjudication of cases, Fleming emphasized the jury system.

African American Jurymen

The jury system is at the core of the American legal system. The feature of the jury in England as in the United States and Australia can be traced to the Anglo-Saxon era. As their forefathers, jurymen in America had an important role in the conviction of criminals. In regard to African Americans, before the Civil War and Reconstruction era, by law, slaves were not permitted to serve on a jury. On the contrary, in plantation governments where the owner was a lawmaker and enforcer, sometimes state laws were overlooked. In fact, each entity in America was under local control. With such decentralization, the observance of laws and the executive power of government officials were not the same. It was not uncommon for local executive officers to empower their faithful slaves with minor local positions in the plantations. As noted, with the observance of local control, African slaves served a jurymen in plantation governments.

Jury System in the Brierfield Plantation

By law, as noted above, African slaves were not authorized to serve in the jury. Contrary to the state law, data collected by Walter L. Fleming shows that Jefferson Davis practiced impartial justice on his plantation. At Brierfield's plantation court, the jury was formed of African Americans.[19] They heard the case and decided the conviction for the accused person. Fleming did not reveal the jury selection procedure observed in the plantation government of President Davis or his brother. Likely, the legal power of the jury was not mentioned. After the conviction of the case, the punishment was administered by an African American.

Correction

The employment of African slaves in correction dates back to the colonial era. During this period, slaves were charged with inflicting physical pain on their brethren in public. This method was used as a general deterrence. At Brierfield, it appears that the system was enforced fairly because the plantation government was inhabited by a large number of African slaves. As such, African slaves were permitted to administer punishment against their own color. According to the wife of the president and other writers, President Davis and his brother prohibited the use of corporal punishment.[20] It appears that African slaves administered justice accordingly.

Perception of Walter L. Fleming on African American Court Officials

In a government where injustice prevails, inhabitants are prone to disobedience or revolt and likely the economic system would also be dsfunctional. At the Brierfield plantation, African slaves charged with the administration of justice believed in the notion of fairness. At the time, African slaves were familiar with discrimination and brutality which they were subjected to in many plantations and towns. They witnessed many cases of mistreatment and oppression. Therefore, they adjudicated cases with impartiality to avoid alienating their own people. As an illustration, Fleming writes that "the Negro took great delight in the workings of the court and showed no disposition to be lenient with criminals."[21] Even though African slaves controlled the judiciary system at the Brierfield plantation, Jefferson Davis had the power to pardon.

Role of Jefferson Davis in the Administration of Punishment

The government of Brierfield Plantation was under the control of Jefferson Davis. He was the executive officer, law maker, and the supreme judge of the court. Likely he was the commander of the militia of his government. With such authority, he reviewed the cases adjudicated by his minor judges. Morris Schaff noted that appeal cases were settled by him.[22] In regard to punishment, Jefferson Davis had the power to make minor changes to the punishment set forth by the jury. Similarly, he had the right to pardon the convicted criminal according to his own will. Granting pardon was a legal procedure accorded to governors in the colony as well as during the American republic. In the United States, the president also had the power to pardon federally convicted criminals.

African Manager or Overseer at the Brierfield Plantation

At the initial establishment of Brierfield plantation, Jefferson Davis employed African slaves for laboring and construction purposes. The slaves were under the control of a manager or overseer. Additionally, the management of the plantation was under the jurisdiction of the managers. After Jefferson Davis's return to Brierfield from military service, for the better management of his plnatation affairs he appointed his friend and companion, James Pemberton, an African slave.

James Pemberton

The relationship between Jeffferson Davis and James Pemberton can be traced back to their childhood when Pemberton was owned by Davis's parents. As children, Davis and Pemberton played together. They probably resided in the same room during this era. Walter L. Fleming noted that Pemberton belonged to the Jefferson family. According to Fleming, Pemberton was owned by Davis's mother. When Davis became a young adult, his mother decided to cede Pemberton to him as a body-servant. This African slave became a loyal friend and servant to him. Morris Schaff notes that "James Pemberton was slave by law, but on the footing with his master, who he had played with as a boy, of a friend and glad Companion."[23] In 1845, when Colonel Jefferson Davis married Miss Howell, Pemberton was also with his master. Colonel Davis traveled with Pemberton by boat to Vicksburg for the wedding.[24]

The accounts of Fleming and Morris Schaff reveals the intensity of the relationship between Jefferson Davis and his African slave, James Pemberton. In 1828, when he was commissioned to war, Pemberton went with his master. He remained with Davis until 1835 when he retired from military duties. During wars, together Davis and Pemberton went on dangerous scouting expeditons and forages. He also cooked for his master and cared for him when he was sick. On one occasion, when Davis was sick, "Pemberton lifted him from his bed and carried him home."[25] Davis and Pemberton were inseparable. During the Mexican War, Davis was appointed Colonel of the 1st Mississippi Rifles. Before his depature for the war, he convened a family council which included Pemberton. At the council, it was decided that Pemberton "should stay and look after the plantation and Jefferson Davis's wife."[26] This trust indicates how Davis valued the character and manner of Pemberton. He believed in him as if he were a family member. Charging him with the care of his wife shows how much Davis trusted Pemberton. Even though Pemberton was a slave, Davis entrusted him with this assignment which could have been given to a free man. At Brierfield, Pemberton was the plantation manager. Pemberton received his managing skills while with his master in the military. He served as Brierfield's manager for many years until his death in 1852. After his death, white managers or overseers were appointed. According to Fleming, some of the white managers did not value the system observed by Jefferson Davis for the administration of his African slaves. As a result, they resigned from their management positions.[27] At Brierfield, white managers were prohibited from inflicting pain on African slaves. This policy was negatively viewed by white managers. Similarly, one of the managers was against the observance of the African American court at the plantation. Even though white managers objected to his policy about African slaves administerng justice, the African American court and the self-governing approach was still in use up to 1862 when the plantation was occupied by the Union forces.

In peace time, African Americans were excluded from law enforcement duties in the South. It appears that it was an established policy. But evidence shows that in plantation governments, some owners were pleased to privilege African slaves with self-governing powers. This was the case at the plantations owned by Jefferson Davis and his brother, Joseph Davis. In these institutions, African slaves controlled components of the criminal justice system. Police, court and correctional duties were under the jurisdiction of African slaves. The owners were entrusted with the appeal cases and pardons.

Notes

1 Sir William Blackstone and Samuel Warren, *Blackstone's Commentaries Sstematically abridged and adopted to the existing state*. W.Maxwell, 1856, pp.88-89.

2 Frederick Douglass, *Narrative of the Life of Frederick Douglass, an American Slave*. Anti-Slavery Office, 1849, pp.5-12.

3 Ibid.

4 Ibid, p.12.

5   Ibid, p.8.

6   Ibid.

7   Carter G. Woodson, *Negro Makers of History*. Wilside Press LLC, 2008, p.113.

8   Ibid.

9   L.B. Castle, *A Treatise on African Colonization in Which the Principles, Objects, and Claims, of that Institution are set*. Scotten & Van Brunt, 1904, p.15.

10 Ulrich Bonnell Philipps, *American Negro Slavery: A Survey of the Supply, Employment and Control of Negro Labor as Determined by the Plantation Regime*. D. Appleton, 1918, p.296.

11 Varina Davis, *Jefferson Davis: Ex-President of the Confederate States of America*, vol.1. Belford Company, 1890, p.48.

12 Ibid.

13 Philipps, 1819, p.296.

14 Davis, 1890, p.174.

15 Ibid.

16 See, Walter L. Fleming. *"Jefferson Davis, the Negroes and the Negro Problem."* The Sewanee Review, vol.16, University of the South, 1908, p.410.

17 Ibid.

18 Morris Schaff, Jefferson Davis: His Life and Personalty, J. W. Luce, 1922, p.30.

19 Davis, 1890, p.175.

20 Davis. The president's wife notes that "corporal punishment was not permitted on "the Brierfield," and was never inflicted except upon conviction of the culpit by a jury of his peers."

21 See Fleming, 1908, p.410.

22 Schaff, 1922, p.30.

23 Ibid, p.19.

24 Ibid, p.47.

25 Ibid, p.27.

26 Ibid, p.58.

27 See Fleming, 1908, p.410.

CHAPTER III

African American Law Enforcers Before the
Civil War in the Northern States

In the northern part of the United States, the history of African Americans in law enforcement can be traced to the little town of Newmarket in New Hampshire. During the Colonial Era, a grandson of an African slave was appointed Justice of the Peace in 1768. Wentworth Cheswell Esq. (also spelled Cheswill), was appointed Justice of the Peace when he was twenty-one years old. As an educated African American, there was no apparent opposition to his appointment as an officer of the court. Cheswell attended Dummer Academy in Byfield, Massachusetts. During Cheswell's tenure at school, the academy was considered a good school for young boys. After completing his education at Dummer, Cheswell was employed as a teacher in the city where he was born. Possibly due to his teaching ability, he was appointed Justice of the Peace of the town. Many authors identify him as the first African American elected to hold a public office in America. In the *New England Historical Genealogy,* he is identified as the "first colored office holder."[1] From the private papers of the late Dr. John Farmer of New Hampshire, historian, genealogist, and member of the American Antiquarian Society, Cheswell is characterized as "a man of considerable information." Cheswell furnished historian Jeremy Belknap with information for his *History of New Hampshire.*[2] Cheswell was appointed coroner November 3, 1785. The information recorded in the *New England Historical Genealogy Society* regarding his position as coroner was the same as recorded in the Provincial and State

Papers of New Hampshire. The president and the council appointed Wentworth Cheswell Esq. coroner of Newmarket in the County of Rockingham in 1785.[3] In the *New Hampshire Annual Register and the United States Calendar* for 1789, he is listed as coroner of Newmarket. In the *New England Historical Genealogy* of 1885, the New Hampshire Annual Register recorded that "there is a tradition that he [Cheswell] was once a slave of one governor Wentworth."[4] Based on other examined documents, there is no evidence that Cheswell was a slave during his life.

In addition to the positions of justice of the peace and coroner, Cheswell was appointed assessor in Newmarket, and held the position for many years. James Hill Fitts and Nellie Plamer George wrote that Cheswell was assessor from 1785 to 1799. This position of assessor was not his last assignment in law enforcement. Cheswell was appointed auditor in the same town. He held the position of auditor of Newmarket in 1786, 1799, and 1801. In 1804, he was entrusted with the same position. Eight years later, he served in the same position, possibly due to his experience in 1814 when he held the position of auditor in Newmarket. With the trust his countrymen had in him, Cheswell was elected moderator in 1801. Three years later, he was once again elected as moderator. He was always re-elected after a few years of being out of office. Again, in 1807 and 1809, he served as moderator. This pattern of Cheswell being re-elected to the same office continued in 1811, 1813, and in 1816. Considering the number of times he was elected to office, it is probable that Cheswell is the longest African American male to serve in law enforcement during the earlier republic and before the war of secession.[5]

As justice of the peace, Cheswell executed the affairs concerning deeds, wills, and other legal papers. He also acted as judge in the trial of causes.[6] In addition to his position as justice of the peace, during the earlier republic, he was appointed selectman in Newmarket.[7] In New England, the selectman regulated the affairs of the town. Bridges, roads, and school constructions were under the jurisdiction of the selectman. In addition to the duties listed above, right to residency in New England's towns was regulated by the selectman of the respective town. Concerning this matter, the selectman made decisions regarding where the intended immigrant desired to settle. Selectmen were elected by the inhabitants of the town. In 1639 in Connecticut, seven people were selected to try small causes, register wills, and administer estates.[8] The selectmen were also called by various other titles. In 1634, they were referred to as "Townsmen" or "Townes Occasions" in Massachusetts.[9] The history of the title of selectmen can be traced back to Massachusetts where the office was first employed by the order of the General Court. The title of selectman was observed in such territories along the eastern seaboard as Massachusetts, Plymouth, Connecticut, New Hampshire, and Maine during the Colonial Era.

Wentworth Cheswell Esq. was from a family which was well-connected in Newmarket and the surrounding era. His father, Hopestill Cheswell, was a reputed master carpenter who settled in Newmarket. In 1746, as a son of an African slave, he petitioned for a bridge over the Saquamscot River. Hopestill Cheswell was the son of Richard Cheswell, a black man who, after marrying a white woman, was liberated from slavery.[10] Currently, the name of Richard's wife is unknown. Hopestill left the best impression in Portsmouth, New Hampshire, where he has been credited with building many historic houses. Wentworth Cheswell died in 1817 after serving his city well. Following his death, his legacy was not forgotten. His son Thomas Cheswell continued in the same honorable path. He was educated at a prestigious school in New London. After his studies, he was appointed selectman and overseer of the poor in Newmarket, a position his father had been elected to many times. Thomas was appointed overseer of the poor in 1815 and selectman in 1816-1817. After five years of serving as selectman, Thomas Cheswell was appointed assessor.[11] He died as his father did in Newmarket. Thomas Cheswell was the son of Wentworth Cheswell and Mary Davis. He was born in 1864, the son of a biracial family. His mother was a white woman and his father was a mulatto. In addition to Thomas' law enforcement positions, he was also much involved in church affairs as a minister.

Just as African Americans performed law enforcement duties in New Hampshire, they performed the same duties in Ohio and Massachusetts. With the formation of political parties, African Americans were always invited to meetings called to launch new political organizations. Attorney John Mercer Langston was invited to the meeting of the Liberty Party in Ohio and in 1855 he was on the ticket of the Liberty Party for the township clerk election.[12] During this period, African Americans had access to the Liberty Party, which was connected to staunch abolitionists. The nomination of Attorney John Mercer Langston was secured by Rev. James H. Fairchild, a professor and president of Oberlin College. Langston's nomination was not opposed by party members, though he doubted he would win the election due to the color of his skin. On the other hand, Professor Fairchild was confident that Langston's nomination would be successful because of the intellectual quality of the attorney. Langston was elected clerk of the town by popular vote. More than likely, he was the first African American to be elected by popular vote in a town of white voters. In Langston's personal book, *From the Virginia Plantation to the National Capital,* he mentions that he was elected clerk of the Township of Brownhelm.[13] On the other hand, Henry Howe, in his *Historical Collection of Ohio* (1847), spoke of Langston as being a clerk of several townships in Ohio.

In 1857, Langston was elected city councilman in Oberlin, Ohio, and was elected to the Board of Education in 1860.[14] At the time of the Langston's election in Ohio, African Americans were franchised in some states in the North—such as in Massachusetts, Vermont, New York, New Hampshire, Rhode Island, and Connecticut. Also in states such as Indiana and Illinois that operated "black codes," laws designated to regulate and control the lives of former slaves, African Americans were permitted to vote. Therefore, highly educated African Americans were sometimes permitted to hold law enforcement positions, such as clerk of the court, justice of the peace, magistrate, and solicitor of the court.

Although educated blacks were sometimes mistrusted and even punished for their intelligence, there were times when they were respected for their knowledge and know-how. Such was the case with John Mercer Langston who performed his political duties well. As a result of his outstanding work-ethic, he was well-respected among public officials and abolitionists. Langston was sometimes invited to speak at anti-slavery meetings. Abolitionists and anti-slavery officials such as Wendell Phillips, William Lloyd Garrison, and John G. Whittier engaged Langston in anti-slavery activities. For example, these men organized a convention at the New York Theatre and invited Langston to be one of the speakers. His presence and input were so significant that the expenses for his travel and accommodations were paid for by the abolitionists. In addition, he was paid $50.00 for his first work as an orator.[15]

Before the election of Langston, Captain William Alexander Leidesdorff, a person of African and Danish descent, was appointed by the Alcade (city attorney) to the city council of San Francisco in 1847. Before his appointment by the Alcade, he was elected to the city council by 109 votes. Leidedorff's opponents, William Glover and William D.M. Howard had 126 and 114 votes, respectively. After Leidedorff's appointment to the city council by the Alcade, the council members chose him to serve the office of town treasurer in 1848. He was also appointed by the town council to be on the committee for public education.[16] In addition to working in local government services, Leidesdorf served as the United States vice-consul at San Francisco. Rudolph M. Lapp, author of *The Blacks in Gold Rush California*, notes that Leidesdorff was a naturalized Mexican citizen. His appointment in 1845 as vice-consul was sanctioned by President Polk. Leidesdorff was well connected to San Francisco from the time of his arrival in the city. He was a businessman who migrated from the West Indies. The first steamboat in San Francisco belonged to Leidesdorff. He brought it with him from Sitka.[17]

In Vermont, Alexander Lucius Twilight, an educated African American, was elected to the House of Representatives in 1836. Edgar Jolls Wiley, editor of the *Catalogue of Officers and Students of Middlebury College in Middlebury, Vermont*, notes that Honorable Alexander Lucuis Twilight was a teacher before his election to the House of Representatives. He taught in Peru, New York, from 1824-1828, Vergennes, Vermont from 1828-1829, and was employed as principal of Orleans County Grammar School from 1829-1831.[18] In the state of Vermont, the institution of slavery was bitterly detested. From when Vermont was inaugurated as the fourteenth state in 1791, slavery was not welcomed nor embraced by government officials. In this state, African Americans enjoyed rights to education, social activities, and limited political obligations.

In 1860, another African American was made a local government official in New Bedford, Massachusetts. Dr. Thomas Bayne, a fugitive slave from Virginia, was elected to the city council in 1860.[19] William Still, author of *The Underground Railroad*, identifies Bayne as a dentist. He had been a slave belonging to Dr. C. F. Martin, who trained Bayne as a dentist. Martin sometimes sent Bayne on medical missions, where he became known for his outstanding professionalism. Dr. Bayne's election to the New Bedford city council is also mentioned in Still's account of people who traveled the Underground Railroad.[20] In New Bedford, colored people were allowed to vote and were eligible to hold office, according to Still, but it is unknown if Bayne was the first person of African descent to be elected in New Bedford, Massachusetts. Colored people in New Bedford were franchised due to the efforts of Paul Cuffee, a Quaker, mariner (sea captain), abolitionist, patriot, and businessman, who is best known for initiating the first back-to-Africa movement for free blacks who wanted to colonize Sierra Leone. Cuffee petitioned the legislature for his right to vote. He presented the argument that paying taxes entitled him to the right to vote. From this reasoning, the legislature decided to enact a law which allowed free people of color, who were tax payers, to be enfranchised like their white counterparts. They would have the same privileges as other citizens.[21] Thus, in New Bedford, Massachusetts people of color would have an impact on the election.[22]

In Boston, Isaac Woodland, a runaway slave from Maryland, was appointed grain inspector. Unlike other escaped slaves, such as Frederick Douglass, Woodland did not exercise his freedom in a free state.

Rather, he settled in Massachusetts, a state that upheld slavery until the Thirteenth Amendment abolished slave ownership and the slave trade. African American abolitionist, journalist, and historian, William Cooper Nell, described Woodland as an inspector who exhibited his duties with honor and was appreciated and respected by the merchants of Boston. With respect to his life in Maryland, Nell did not comment whether Woodland was educated or not. But as grain inspector, it was possible he was self-educated, unlike many other slaves of his time. Historically, slaves appointed to local government jobs before the Civil War were formally educated to some extent, and they articulated the English language with authority.

Macon Bolling Allen, an African American who resided in Massachusetts, was appointed as justice of the peace on April 21, 1847 by Governor George N. Briggs, a Whig Party member. Allen was re-appointed in 1854 by Governor Emory Washburn, another Whig Party member.[23] Justice of the Peace Allen was the first admitted black lawyer to practice law in Maine and Massachusetts. According to Wilson Armistead, author of *A Tribute for the Negro*, "Macon Allen successfully passed the time ordeal of a rigid examination and held the office of justice of the peace for the Middlesex County, United States."[24] Upon his admittance to the Suffolk Bar, Allen was fully approved by Honorable John Palfrey and distinguished Harvard University law professor, Simon Greenleaf.[25]

In the same state where Allen was appointed justice of the peace, Governor Briggs also appointed Robert Morris, a black lawyer, magistrate in Essex County. Morris was possibly the first African American to serve in this office when he began his term in 1852.[26] It was on Thursday, June 27, 1850, that Morris had been admitted to the bar in Boston before the members of the Suffolk County Bar. At this meeting, he was permitted to practice as counselor and attorney of the Circuit and District Courts of the United States.[27] As an attorney and abolitionist, he defended many cases of fugitive slaves with the assistance of Honorable Charles Sumner. Morris volunteered as counsel in the case of Anthony Burns, a fugitive slave from Virginia who escaped to Boston, Massachusetts. Morris worked with Sumner in the case of *Sarah C. Roberts v. The City of Boston* (December 4, 1849). The case of Sarah C. Roberts was based on separate schools for black and white students. Benjamin Roberts did not want his daughter, Sarah, to attend the school on Belknap Street established for black students. The founder of the school was Prince Hall, a colored abolitionist living in Boston. When Sarah applied to a white school, she was denied. Robert Roberts, Sarah's father, disagreed with the refusal to admit his daughter, so he sued the city of Boston. From this case, a historical and monumental decision was made. The Massachusetts legislature declared that "in determining the qualifications of schools to be admitted into any public school or any District School in this Commonwealth, no distinction shall be made on account of the race, color, or religious opinions of the applicant or scholar." The decision resulting from *Roberts v. City of Boston* case was the first time in the United States that "equality before the law was introduced in the legal system."[28] Sumner noted that equality before the law was not a common law discussion [nor was it a discussion] borrowed from the English law.[29]

In 1861, Dr. John Sweet Rock, a fugitive Negro who studied medicine and law, was appointed justice of the peace to Suffolk County, Massachusetts by Governor John Andrew and the council. He was the justice in Boston for seven years, where he also acted as an abolitionist and practiced medicine. Upon the motion of T.K. Lothrop, Esq., Rock was examined by the Supreme Court of Massachusetts and was permitted to practice law in all the courts in the state.[30] From the account of William Wells Brown, abolitionist, historian, and prolific writer, Rock was permitted to practice in all courts within the jurisdiction of the United States and the Supreme Court in Washington, D.C.[31]

George B. Vashon, abolitionist, lawyer, scholar, poet, and first black graduate of Oberlin College in Ohio, was admitted to the New York Bar after examination. Ultimately, Vashon became an attorney, solicitor, and counselor of the Supreme Court for the state of New York, according to Wilson Armistead, author of A *Tribute for the Negro*.[32] Vashon was familiar with the thinkers of the British legal system. He was acquainted with persons in the law profession such as Sir Edward Coke, who defended the supremacy of the common law over claims of royal prerogative, an argument which greatly influenced the development of English law and the English Constitution and Sir William Blackstone, English barrister, judge, and Tory politician whose reputation is largely based on his commentaries concerning English law which culminated in his publication of *An Analysis of the Laws of England* (1756). These learned British men, experts on England's common law, greatly impacted English law. In addition, their writings had much influence on the American, Canadian, and Australian legal systems.

In addition to law enforcement duties, African Americans were employed as jailors. For example, professor and author Marvin Dulaney asserts that Ellidgea Poindexter and Douglass C. Butler worked as jailors in the city jail in New Orleans, Louisiana. These two African Americans served as turnkeys (jailors) for several years in the city jail.[32] Little is known about these two African Americans. It appears that Poindexter and Butler were free men of color, for, if they were slaves, they would not have been employed as jailors.

In Northern states, a limited number of free educated African Americans held law enforcement positions such as justice of the peace and city council membership. Data does not show that they were appointed as policemen. Even though abolitionists in Northern states, and especially the New England regions, advocated for the liberation of African slaves from bondage, they did not fight for the inclusion of these people in the police force.

Notes

1   *"Notes and Queries,"* The New England Historical Genealogy, 1885, p.192.

2   Ibid.

3   See Provincial and State papers, vol.20, New Hampshire, Authority of the legislature of New Hampshire, 1891, p.558.

4   The New England Historical genealogy, 1885, p.192.

5   See James Hill Fitts, History of Newfield, New Hampshire, 1638 – 1911, The Rumford Press, 1912, pp.290 – 294, the Granite Monthly: a New Hampshire Magazine devoted to history and Nellie Palmer George, 1916, see the Mansion House of Wentworth Cheswill, p.203.

6   The Granite Monthly and Otis Grant Hammon, J.N. McClintock, 1906, p.50.

7   Ibid.

8   See Johns Hopkins University Studies Historical and Political Science, vol.4, 1889, p.75.

9   Edward Hartwell Savage, *A Chronological History of the Boston Watch and Police.* The Author. 1865, p.12. Savage notes that "on September 1, 1634, nine Townes Occasions were chosen for superintending the local affairs of the town."

10   Valerie Cunningham and Mark J. Sammons, *Black Portsmouth: Three centuries of African – American heritage*, UPNE, 2004, p.32.

11   See Fitts, 1912, p, 140 Fitts relates a brief biography of Elder Thomas Cheswell, the son of Esq. Wentworth Cheswell and Mary Davis.

12   John Mercer Langston, *From the Virginia plantation to the National capital*, American Publishing Company, 1894, pp.143 – 145.

13   Ibid.

14   Ibid, p.168.

15   Ibid, p.145.

16   See Dellilah Leontium Beasley, *The negro Trail Blazers of California.* Times Mirror Printing and Binding House, 1919, p.107. See also, the Sans Francisco Municipal Reports, 1911, p.1288.

17   Frank Soule, John H. Gihon, and Jim Nisbet, *The Annal of San Francisco: Containing a summary of the history of . . . California, and a complete history of – its Great City, to which are added Biographical memoirs of some prominent citizens,* D. Appleton & Company, 1855, p.196- 201.

18   Dr. Thomas Bayne, an African American, see Virginia General Assembly. Dr. Martin Luther King Kr. Memorial Commission, Short Biographies of African American legislators in Virginia.

19   Dr. Thomas Bayne, an African American, see *William Still The Underground Rail Road: A record of facts, authentic narratives, letter, &c.,* Porter & Coates, 1872, p.254.

20   Nell, 1855, p.77.

21   Ibid, p.112.

22 Clay J. Smith, Jr. Emancipation: *The making of black lawyer, 1844 – 1944,* University of Pennsylvania Press, 1999, p.94.

23 Macon Allen, see *Wilson Armistead A tribute for the Negro,* Harned – New York, 1848, p141.

24 Nell, 1855, p.328.

25 Smith Jr., 1999, p.99.

26 George Washington Williams, *History of the Negro in America, 1619 to 1880.* G.P. Putnam's Sons, 1883, p.123.

27 Charles Sumner, *Charles Sumner; His Complete Works,* vol.3. Lee & Shepard, 1900, p.51. See also Sarah C. Roberts vs. The City of Boston on the Reports of Cases Argued and Determined in the Supreme Judicial Court of the Commonwealth of Massachusetts, vol.59. Litle, Brown, 1853, pp.198-201.

28 Charles Sumner *The work of works of Charles Sumner,* Lee and Shephard, 1870, p.327.

29 Brown, 1863, p.266.

30 Ibid, p.295.

31 George B. Vashon, see W. Irwin, 1848, p.140.

32 Dulaney, 1996, p.10.

CHAPTER IV

The Emancipation Proclamation and the Employment of African Americans

The emancipation and military enlistment of African descendants were administered by proclamations, acts, and orders established by the American officials and generals in the fields. In 1861, General Butler freed African slaves who came to the Union lines by using the legal term "contraband of war." His reasoning was approved by the Secretary of War, Simon Cameron, who in May, 1861, advised him to keep fugitive slaves in the Union lines and use them for government work. In the meantime, Secretary of War Simon Cameron told General Butler to keep an account of the labor performed by the contraband.[1] Slaves who escaped to Fortress Monroe in the beginning of the war were liberated by General Butler because they were the slaves of Colonel Mallory.[2] The first contrabands received by General Butler became free from bondage, and received protection from the United States government. The policy employed by General Butler was continued by Major General Wool, his successor. At Fortress Monroe, Major General Wool ordered that "all colored persons called contraband employed by officers or others within his command, must be furnished with substance by their employers, and paid, if males, not less than $8.00; if females, not less than $4.00 per month; and all able bodied colored persons, not employed as aforesaid will be immediately put to work in the engineer's or the Quartermaster's Department." He also directed that the compensation of contrabands working for the government should be $5 to $10 per month, with soldier's ration.[3] The orders show the earliest employment of African Americans in the service of the United States as well as limited civil rights protections during the Civil War. Moreover, slavery was no longer enforced in the camps under the control of the Union. It appears that African Americans in the camp of the Union were protected by the Law of Nations because they were identified as contraband. On the other hand, the part of the United States occupied by the Confederates were considered a foreign nation during the war.

In Missouri, Major General John C. Fremont proclaimed the liberation of African Americans in 1861. According to his proclamation, the properties of people who took arms against the United States were subject to confiscation and their slaves were declared free."[4] This proclamation was nullified by President Lincoln, and Major General Fremont was transferred to a different department. By revoking the proclamation of General Fremont, President Lincoln attempted to appease Confederate states officials by indicating that he was not abolishing the institution of slavery which was dear to them.[5] Even though the proclamation was revoked, some African slaves were freed by General Fremont's proclamation. The slaves of General Thomas L. Snead were emancipated through the proclamation of General Fremont. Frank Lewis and Iram Reed, the slaves of General Thomas L. Snead, received their freedom in 1861 through the proclamation of General Fremont. According to the manumission deeds, Frank Lewis and Iram Reed were free from the service of General Thomas L. Snead who took arms against the United States.[6] The emancipation deed of Lewis was legal and recognizable by all people as well as all court jurisdictions.

When General Fremont was moved from the Department of the South, General Hunter in South Carolina followed the same policy of emancipating African slaves through his proclamation. After the said proclamation, he formed a regiment of people of color which was disbanded thereafter. Many fugitive slaves were also employed in the service of the United States. General Hunter declared them free without regard to the revocation of Fremont's emancipation by President Abraham Lincoln. He also welcomed the entrance of African

Americans to the Union lines. The policy of General Hunter in regard to African Americans was directed by his own conviction as well as the anti-slavery Massachusetts officials.

General Hunter, who commanded the Department of the South with his headquarters in Hilton Head in South Carolina, in 1862 proclaimed that "the three states of Georgia, Florida, and South Carolina, comprising the Military Department of the South, having deliberately declared themselves no longer under the protection of the United States of America, and having taken up arms against the said United States, it became a military necessity to declare them under martial law. Slavery and martial law in a free country are altogether incompatible. The person in these three states, Georgia, Florida, and South Carolina, therefore held as slaves, are therefore declared forever free."[7] His proclamation was also revoked by President Lincoln. After the passage of his proclamation, General Hunter formed a military regiment of people of African descent which was disbanded by the order of the president.

General Lyon, who freed his slaves voluntarily, noted that "he had liberated his own slaves, and was determined to set free all the slaves of any other person that might come in his way."[8] It is unknown whether or not he liberated slaves that were in contact with him. On the other hand, Colonel Jennison noted that he would not stop fighting in the war until the last slave in the United States was free."[9] Moreover, Colonel Jennison, who disliked slavery, stressed that "the last dollar and the last slave of rebels were to be taken and turned over to the General Government."[10] The perception of these generals in regard to slaves was the same as anti-slavery officials and abolitionists. Most of these generals had long been conviced that slavery must be abolished in the United States. The New England generals such as Phelps, Fremont, Jennison, and Hunter did not value slave labor, but only free labor. The liberation of African slaves was also used as a psychological weapon to demoralize their masters. It seemed that during the Civil War, slaveholders feared the employment of black men in the military anticipating reprisal or revenge.

At the beginning of the war, there were many approaches taken towards African slaves. Their freedom, as well as their inclusion in the military of the Union or the militia, was managed according to the convictions of the government officials and generals. Among government officials, as well as generals, there were pro-slavers, Union loyalists, and abolitionist Union supporters. It seems that pro-slavers did not want the advocacy of the abolition of the institution of slavery by either party during the the execution of the Civil War. On the other hand, Union loyalists only supported the causes of the federal government and did not focus on the institution of slavery during the same war. On the contrary, abolitionist generals and government officials were fighting for the cause of the Union and the abolition of slavery. To illustrate, General Dix, a Union supporter, in his proclamation to the people of Accomac and North Hampton assured them that by the special directives given to them, "they were not to interfere with the condition of any domestic servitude."[11] On the contrary, Colonel Jennison, a firm New England abolitionist, believed that the organized regiment was not for political effect, but for fighting purposes and freedom."[12] The fight for freedom which the general stressed was the liberation of African slaves in America. His perception was supported by government officials such as Charles Sumner, Henry Wilson, both Massachusetts senators, and Governor Andrew of Massachusetts.[13]

Among the supporters of slavery, at their meeting in Frankfort, Kentucky, Union members noted that it was unconstitutional for the president or any other person to interfere with the institution of domestic slavery.[14] The President of the United States, during his inauguration speech, declared that he "had no purpose, directly, or indirectly, to interfere with the institution of slavery in the states where it exists." He also went on to note that he "believed he did not have lawful right to do so, and he had no inclination to do so."[15] Even during the Civil War, President Lincoln declared that the war was not for the liberation of African slaves, but for the preservation of the Union. He also believed that constitutionally, he was not permitted to free Africans from slavery. Therefore, the freeing of African slaves was not part of the policy of his administration. In addition, it appeared that during the Civil War, there was no planned policy for the liberation of African Americans. Generals in the field acted according to their best possible interests until Congress passed a law which declared that escaped slaves employed for the construction of fortification or building military work for the rebels, should be free when they enter Union lines. The bill was sponsored by Senator Lyman Trumbull in a special session on July 4, 1861, and became law by order of President Lincoln on the 6th of August, 1861. The Act of Congress approved on the 6th of August was entitled "An act to confiscate property used for the insurrectionary purposes."[16]

Before and after the passage of the law of August 6, 1861, sometimes African Americans who came to the Union lines were sent back to their masters by the generals. Even after the passage of the law restricting the return of slaves, some generals continued to send them back to their masters. Major General Halleck who replaced General Fremont in the command in Missouri issued an order excluding African Americans from Union lines. His order No. 3 reads as follows: "It has been represented that important information, respecting the number and condition of our forces, is conveyed to the enemies by means of fugitive slaves who are admitted within our lines. In order to remedy this evil, it is directed that no such persons be hereafter permitted to enter the lines of any camp, or of any forces on the march; and that any now within such lines be immediately excluded."[17] In his Order 13, General Halleck notes that "it does not belong to the military to decide upon the relation of master and slave. Such questions must be settled by the civil courts. No fugitive slaves will, therefore, be admitted within our lines or camps, except when specially ordered by the general commanding."[18] Major General Halleck did not obey the Act of Congress approved on August 6, 1861, which ordered the protection of fugitive slaves and forbade their return to their masters. The orders of General Halleck demonstrate that the liberation of African slaves was not part of his mission during the war either as strategy or as a way to demoralize the enemies. It appeared that his reasoning was not in the favor of the emancipation of slaves. Probably, General Halleck did not have the same convictions as abolitionist generals from the New England region, or he followed the approach of President Lincoln which was that the preservation of the Union was the sole reason for the Civil War. Possibly, General Halleck had some sort of relationship with slaveholders in other states in the north or in the south. General Halleck was not the only high ranking military official who opposed the entrance of African Americans in the Union lines. There were other generals who thought similarly.

The difficulties of managing the affairs of escaped slaves happened in Louisiana when a big influx of them approached Union lines. General Butler did not know which approach to take because the government did not have a planned policy regarding their fate. James Parton notes that the president told him verbally that "the government was not yet prepared to announce a Negro policy. He must get along with the Negro question the best way he could and try to manage so that neither abolitionists nor conservatives would find in this act occasions for clamor."[19] In addition, President Lincoln told General Butler "to run the machine as he found it."[20] This statement means that General Butler was obligated to find the best way possible to avoid infuriating pro-slavers and abolitionists. In like manner, he was also instructed to appease African Americans as best as he could. While General Butler followed the appeasing strategy employed by President Lincoln and his executive officers in Louisiana, General Phelps, an abolitionist from Massachusetts, desired to employ African Americans as soldiers. But for General Butler, the idea of arming African Americans was left to the president. He preferred employing African Americans for cutting wood. General Phelps did not feel comfortable giving escaped African slaves work that seemed like slavery. As a result, he resigned from his military service.[21]

African Americans also believed in their own liberation. Those who joined the army fought for their freedom from bondage. For that reason, they were loyal to the cause of the Union and fought fiercely hoping that the fall of the Confederate regime in the South would be the beginning of their freedom. Moore, a slave was among those who felt that fighting for the cause of the Union was important for their liberation. According to James Mckaye, Messrs Leeds' slave was the first person killed during the Civil War. Mr. Moore, the

African American slave noted to his family that: "I know I shall fall, but you will be free."[22] African Americans were also motivated to join the army because those who escaped to the hand of the Generals of the Union were treated fairly and were subjected to some freedoms. The proclamation of General Hunter and Fremont were indications that the liberation of African slaves in America was one of the strategies to weaken the rebels during the Civil War. Moreover, generals employing African slaves without the consent of government officials set a precedent showing that abolitionist generals were determined to liberate African slaves and defeat the Confederate Army. Since slaves were aware of this, they volunteered information and other services for the cause of the Union. They established an open relationship with Union officials and served them with loyalty. On the other hand, loyal abolitionist generals took care of them and advocated for their protection. African Americans, such Mr. Frederick Douglass, advocated for the inclusion of African Americans for the cause of the Union from the start of the war, but his and other African Americans' efforts were fruitless at the start of the war.

Before the proclamation of President Lincoln, the employment of African Americans for the service of the United States was completed by generals in the field. Generals such as David Hunter, Thomas Wentworth Higginson, John W. Phelps, Rufus Saxton, and Lieutenant Colonel Trowbridge formed unofficial regiments of people of color in 1862. The official authorized regiments of people of color were formed by the order of Congress in 1862 with the passage of the Second Confiscation and Militia Act of July 17, 1862. This act permitted the president to allow African Americans to be used in the army according to their needs and the public's welfare.[23] On August 25, 1862, the War Department was authorized to organize a regiment of African American volunteer laborers to a number not exceeding fifty thousand. They were to be mustered in the service of the United States.[24] This regiment was mandated to guard the plantations and settlements occupied by the United States. They were also required to protect the inhabitants from captivity and murder by the rebels.[25]

Unlike Generals Hunter and Fremont, in 1863 President Lincoln proclaimed the Emancipation for the liberation of people of African descent in the rebellious states, including their enrollment in the army and the navy of the United States. Before the Emancipation Proclamation of 1863, President Lincoln gave a warning proclamation on September 22, 1862 which historians call the first emancipation. This emancipation revealed the intention of the president in regard to war strategy. With the intensity and the magnitude of the war, the president thought it better not to please rebels. Perhaps, he found that pleasing the rebels did not bring about change in their behavior in regard to the unification of the country and the termination of the war. As a result, he pronounced his first proclamation advising the rebels to give up arms or endure the consequences of the war. The president knew how the rebels weighed their African slaves. Therefore, as a military strategy, liberating African slaves as well as enlisting them in the United States army was beneficial for the Union. In like manner, the rebels were to be weakened by the loss of their African slaves who assisted them in many ways during the war. African slaves took care of the families of their masters while they went to war, and provided money as well food to the rebels. In 1862, when the dynamic of the war was not in favor of the Union, the president was not reserved as before and pronounced his first Emancipation Proclamation. His first Emancipation Proclamation reads as follows:

"That on the first day of January in the year of our Lord one thousand eight hundred and sixty-three, all persons held as slaves within any state or designated part of state, the people whereof shall then be in rebellion against the United States, shall be then, thenceforward, and forever free: and the Executive Government of the United States, including the military and naval authority thereof, will recognize and maintain the freedom of such persons, and will do not act or acts to repress such persons, or any of them, in any efforts they may make for their actual freedom, I further declare and make known, that such person of suitable condition, will be received into the armed service of the United States to garrison forts, positions, stations, and other places, and to man vessels of all sorts in said service."[26]

The rebels were not receptive to the warning of President Lincoln and continued to fight against the Union. It appeared that they did not care much about the warning of the president because they did not believe that he had the constitutional power to enforce his proclamation. Furthermore, the rebels were determined to win the war at any cost. Therefore, President Lincoln's warning was not taken seriously. On the other hand, President Lincoln found a pretext to liberate and enlist escaped slaves protected in the Union camps. The idea of enlisting African slaves was discussed by the president in his meeting with some officials in his cabinet. In Francis Bicknell Carpenter's book, *The Inner Life of Abraham Lincoln; Six Months at the White House*, we found that Secretary Seward advised President Lincoln to postpone his decision regarding the liberation of the slaves held in the rebel states. The reason for postponing the liberation of slaves was as follows: "I approve the proclamation, but I question the expediency of its issue at this juncture. The depression of the public mind, consequent upon our related reverses, is so great that I fear the effect of so important a step. It may be viewed as the last measure of an exhausted government stretching forth its hands to Ethiopia instead of Ethiopia stretching forth her hands to the government."[27] Secretary Seward desired that the proclamation be correlated with military success instead of issuing when the army suffered many defeats. On the other hand, the secretary believed that the loss of territories, properties, and human lives was fresh in the public mind and liberating African slaves wouldn't be supported by the majority of the American public.[28] Furthermore, while the Union army suffered many defeats, emancipating African slaves made it seem that the government was incapable of winning the war without external support. The Secretary of War's perception of the Emancipation Proclamation may have been possibly supported by the inner circle of the president.

Secretary Seward's idea was well received by President Lincoln who responded that "the wisdom of the view of the Secretary of State struck him with very great force. It was an aspect of the care that, in all his thought upon the subject, he had entirely overlooked."[29] President Lincoln was motivated to issue the liberation of African slaves due to their inclusion in the military, and the various acts of the United States Congress which freed some of them. Moreover, African slaves in the city of Washington were freed by an act of Congress sponsored by Senator Charles Wilson of Massachusetts in 1862.[30] Therefore, the president was comfortable proclaiming their liberation which was partially approved by abolitionists and other Northerners. As the proclamation was a military tactic to defeat the rebellion, the president knew that abolitionists and Union loyalists would not take issue with the enlistment of African Americans in the military. Since the rebels did not comply with the first proclamation, the President delivered a second one on January 1, 1863 which reads:

Whereby, in virtue of the power vested in him as "commander in chief of the Army and Navy of the United States in time of actual armed rebellion against the authority and government of the United states, and as a fit and necessary war measure for suppressing the said rebellion," he designates as being in rebellion the states of Arkansas, Texas, Louisiana (thirteen counties excepted), Mississippi, Alabama, Florida, Georgia, South Carolina, North Carolina, and Virginia (the forty-eight counties of West Virginia, and seven others, excepted), and ordered and declared.

"That all persons held as slaves within said designated states, and parts of states, are and henceforward shall be free; and that the Executive Government of the United States, including the military and naval authorities thereof, will recognize and maintain the freedom of said persons. And I hereby enjoin upon the people so declared to be free, to abstain from all violence, unless in necessary self-defense; and I recommend to them that in all cases where allowed, they labor faithfully for reasonable wages. And I further declare and make known that such persons, of suitable condition, will be received into the armed service of the United States to garrison forts, positions, stations, and other places, and to man vessels of all sorts in said service. And upon this act sincerely, believed to be an act of justice, warranted by the Constitution upon military necessity, I invoke the considerate judgment of mankind, and the gracious favour of Almighty God."[31]

The emancipation of slaves, which President Lincoln proclaimed, was also proposed by Senator Pemeroy of Kansas. On July 16, 1861, the senator introduced a bill in the senate declaring that "slavery should be abolished in all states which rebelled against the government of the United States."[32] The bill did not have much support at the beginning of the war because the emancipation of African slaves was not a policy of the Lincoln administration. Unlike Senator Pemeroy of Kansas, Hon. Thaddeus Stevens advocated for the enlistment of people of color in the army to fight for the preservation of the Union at the start of the war. In July 1861, he declared that "slavery caused the rebellion: that there could be "no solid and permanent peace and Union" in the republic so long as slavery existed within it; that slaves were "used by the rebels as essential means of supporting and protracting the war," and that by the law of nations it was "right to liberate the slaves of the enemy to weaken his power." He went on to order that "the president be requested to declare free, and to direct all generals and officers in command to order freedom to, all slaves who shall leave their masters or shall aid in quelling this rebellion."[33] The order of Hon. Thaddeus Stevens was the first of the propositions to support the liberation of the enemy's slaves as well as their enlistment for the quelling of the rebellion. For political or war strategies, the president and his administration did not consider Hon. Thaddeus' logic of thinking regarding the liberation of slaves and their enlistment in the Union army. Hon. Thaddeus Stevens also invoked international law so that the liberation and the enlistment of African Americans in the army would not be considered unconstitutional. According to the United States Constitution, the president was not authorized to call upon citizens to quell a rebellion in the states. It also appeared that public opinion was not in favor of calling upon people of the African race to fight for the cause of the Union. Hon. Thaddeus Stevens indicated genuine interest in the cause of people of color. He was troubled to hear that General Halleck was ordering the expulsion of African Americans who came to the Union lines. Hoping to avoid the return of slaves who came to the Union camps, Hon. Thaddeus Stevens requested the president to order General Halleck to withdraw his order which prohibited the entrance of African Americans to the Union camps.[34]

African Americans who disliked the institution of slavery were ready to fight for liberty and the preservation of the Union when the president first called for volunteers in 1861. In Boston, black people had a meeting for that purpose. William Wells Brown, an African American author and Civil War veteran, states that African Americans' requests for serving in the army was turned down by government officials. In the meeting, the committee declared as follows: "Resolved, that our feelings urge us to say to our countrymen that we are ready to stand by and defend the Government as the equals of its white defenders; to do so with our lives, our fortunes, and our sacred honor, for the sake of freedom and as good citizens; and we ask you to modify your laws, that we may enlist, that full scope may be given to the patriotic feelings burning in the colored man's breast."[35] This information was collected by Mr. William Wells Brown during the Colored Men's meeting in Boston. Like the senators and congressmen, people of the African race requested an amendment of United States laws so that they could be enlisted in the army. At the start of the Civil War, black people believed in having the same share as white people for the sake of freedom. Equality and freedom were the two concepts that were advocated by the supporters of the Civil Rights Bill and the Fourteenth Amendment.

Lincoln's Emancipation Proclamation revolutionized the entrance of African Americans in the army and in the service of the United States. Governor John Andrew of Massachusetts was the first of the state government officials to receive permission from the war department in 1863 to form a regiment of people of color. He formed the 54th Massachusetts Volunteer regiment. The proclamation of President Lincoln increased African American enlistment in the army and the navy. Like in Massachusetts, regiments of people of color were formed in many states of the Union. In 1863, after President Lincoln's proclamation, the government formed a new policy in regard to the employment of people of African descent in the army and the Navy. In order for the new policy to materialize, Lorenzo Thomas, the Adjutant General of the United States army was sent to Mississippi in March, 1863, to initiate and supervise the recruitment of black soldiers as well as the commission officers of the said regiments. General Thomas Lorenzo visited many cities where African Americans were gathered in areas such as Memphis and Helena. During his enlistment visits, he strongly emphasized the emancipation of slaves proclaimed by the president of the United States.[36] With the efforts of General Lorenzo Thomas, General Banks, and others, many regiments of people of color were formed. The War Department also established many recruiting stations in states such as in Maryland, Missouri, and Tennessee. In addition to the formation of black regiments, the Bureau of Colored Regiments was also established. The bureau was under the control of the adjutant general's office in Washington. The object of the bureau was the recording of all affairs regarding the organization of black troops.[37]

The effect of the war was so dire among blacks and other whites who were loyal to the Union. Most of them were scattered in the Union camps and lines seeking protections and accommodations. For the civil rights of refugees and freed slaves, Hon. Trumbull of Illinois proposed a bill for the establishment of the bureau for the relief of said people which were to be fed and clothed by the government of the United States under the leadership of the generals. With this influx of freed slaves and loyal refugees in military camps, on March 3, 1865, the United States Congress enacted a law with a special object: the establishment of a bureau for the care of freed slaves and refugees of the Civil War.[38] The bureau was called the Freedmen's Bureau. This bureau helped freedmen find employment and also assisted them with making contracts. The bureau was the first established office which enforced the civil rights of freed slaves and loyal refugees who lived under the threat of the Confederate Army. The bureau was administered by a commissioner and assistant commissioners. According to Congress, the mandate of the bureau was for one year. In 1866, at the end of the mandate of the bureau, the United States Congress extended its services after the veto of President Andrew Johnson.[39]

The emancipation of slaves was not throughout the entire United States. The president only liberated the slaves residing in the rebel states listed in the proclamation. Those who lived in the loyal states were still slaves under their masters. Even in the state of Louisiana, which was rebellious against the United States, the African slaves in the parishes controlled by loyal supporters and foreigners were not freed. They still lived under the control of their masters. In Parishes such as St. Bernard, Placquemines, Jefferson, St. John, St. Charles, St. James, Assension, Assumption, Terre Bonne, Lafourche, St. Mary, St. Martin, and Orleans, including the city of New Orleans, Africans remained slaves of their masters.[40] James Parton, who wrote about the administration of General Butler in the Gulf, states that slaves in some parishes that were under the control of the United States, were freed by the said general. In addition, General Butler invoked international law for the liberation of slaves who resided in the parishes which belonged to foreign-born people. In the French parishes, the French law was enforced and in the British parishes, the British law was also employed. The French law stipulated that "no French citizens in Louisiana could lawfully own a slave." On the other hand, the English law forbade the owning of slaves by British subjects in any part of the world, under penalties. With these laws, General Butler was able to liberate colored slaves who resided in the foreign parishes.[41] He applied international law for their liberation.[42] The invocation of the Law of Nations in liberating African slaves under the areas occupied by the French and English was meant to legalize such actions and avoid any legal disputes.

The proclamation of President Lincoln was not taken with more weight in Confederate states such as Kentucky, Georgia, Louisiana, Mississippi, Alabama, and South Carolina. In Kentucky, where some officials were loyal to the Union, they believed that the emancipation of slaves would not affect the state. According to the Act of Congress of March 1865, African slaves freed themselves by escaping and others were freed by enlisting in the army. The families of slaves who enlisted in the United States army were also liberated.[43] Similarly, in the state of South Carolina, Georgia, and Mississippi, the institution of slavery was not abolished after President Lincoln's emancipation proclamation. According to the report of Carl Churz and Ulysses Grant, in Southern states, Africans were social slaves, but not their master's slaves.[44] By social slaves, it appeared that they were considered second class citizens and did not have any kind of rights whatsoever. The report also indicated that in the localities where the army was virtually absent, slavery was kept intact in the South. On several plantations located where the war was not fought, masters continued to slave Africans there.[45] The investigation of Carl Churz and Ulysses Grant in the South revealed many abuses which African Americans were subjected to at the hands of their former masters and other southern subjects.

President Lincoln's emancipation proclamation was a military necessity. The abolition of slavery in the United States through a constitutional amendment was first proposed by Hon. James M. Ashley on December 14, 1863. Hon. James Wilson of Iowa also prepared a detailed joint resolution to amend the State Constitution for the abolition of slavery.[46] Unlike the other recommendations, Constitutional lawyers such as Lyman Trumbull preferred the abolition of slavery by amending the Constitution of the United States. Senator Lyman Trumbull of Illinois, who was the chairman of the judiciary committee, assisted with the framing of the 13th Amendment which abolished slavery in the entire United States and proposed an amendment to the Constitution for the same purpose. As noted before, slavery in the United States was not fully abolished by Lincoln's proclamations. Therefore, the 13th Amendment was the sole mechanism employed by government officials to abolish slavery in the entire United States.

During the Civil War, Union soldiers, as well as President Abraham Lincoln, invoked the proclamation for the purposes of enlisting African slaves in the rank of the United States army. Among Union soldiers, General Fremont and Butler proclaimed the liberation of African slaves belonging to owners who took weapons against the United States for military necessity. Like the general listed above, President Lincoln did the same. The proclamations of Fremont and Butler were nullified by the president. In addition to the proclamations, self-liberated African Americans joined the rank of the Union in many capacities such as spies, scouts, guides, and informants. The enlistment of African slaves as a military neccessity was championed by many lawmakers before Lincoln's proclamation.

Notes

1 Horace Greeley, *The American Conflict: A history of the Great Rebellion in the United States*, 1860 – 65, p.238.

2 Ibid.

3 Ibid, p.240 For information about Col. Mallory and his three slaves see also the book of John Stevens Cabot Abbott, The History of the Civil War in America, vol. I, H. Bill, 1863, p.136. Abbot tells us that three slaves went to the Union camp to seek protection. Col. Mallory and General Butler knew each other before the commencement of the Civil War. They were members of the same political party. Abbott notes that at the Charleston and Baltimore Conventions, both men did not share cordial words with each other. When Col. Mallory sent his agent to General Butler reclaiming his slaves, the general told him that African Americans, which the agent called properties, were employed to destroy the lives and property of citizens of the United States. General Butler also went on to note that the agent that these Negroes, when able bodied are, of great importance, without them, those batteries could not have been erected, at least for many weeks. The argument of General Butler was made as a justification why he identified escaped slaves as "Contrabands" so that they would be protected according to the law of nations. Edith Ellen Ware, who edited the Political Opinion in Massachusetts during Civil War and Reconstruction, vo.74. issue 2, 1916 says that the theory of contraband which was raised early in national affairs by Butler and Fremont was approved as practical tactics. By analyzing the expression of Ware, we can say the contraband was employed during the war so that African Americans would be liberated to support the Union militarily.

4 Harrison Anthony Trexler, *Slavery in Missouri, 1804 – 1865*, Johns Hopkins, 1914, p.232 For the proclamation of Major General Fremont, Major General Fremont's Proclamation reads as follows "All persons who shall be taken with arms in their hands within these line shall be tried by court martial, and if found guilty, will be shot. The property, real and personal, of all persons in the state of Missouri, who shall take up arms against the United States, or who shall be directly proven to have taken active part with their enemies in the field, is declared to be confiscated to the public use, and their slaves, if any they have, are hereby declared free men." See William Wells Brown, The Negro in the American Rebellion, 1867, p.70.

5 President Lincoln said, "If the Union could be saved with slavery preserved, he would thus save it." See J.S. MCNeily, *War and Reconstruction*

in Mississippi: 1863 – 1890, Publications of the Mississippi Historical Society, vol.2, 1918, p.169.

6   William Wells Brown, *The Negro in the American Rebellion: His Heroism and His Fidelity*, Lee & Shepard, 1867, p.71.

7   Ibid.

8   Thoma Wallace, *Knox Camp – Fire and Cotton-field: Southern Adventure in Time of War*, Bulock and Company, 1865, p.220.

9   Frank Moore, *A Diary of American Events*, 1862, p.377.

10 Evert Augustus Duyckinck, *National History of the war and Naval. Founded on official and other authentic documents*, Johnson, Fry, 1861, p.171.

11 Moore, 1862, p.377.

12 Ibid, p.377.

13 Benson John Lossing tells us that "National Senate Henry Wilson, and Charles Sumner were Known in every part of the Union as the most able and uncompromising opponents of the slave system; and its Governor at that time John A. Andrew was an earnest co-worker with them in the cause of the final emancipation of the slaves within the borders of the Republic. See B. J. Lossing, *Pictorial History of the Civil War in the United States of America*, 1866, p.202.

14 Ibid, p.415.

15 Greeley, 1867, p.244.

16 Ibid. 241.

17 Ibid.

18 Horace Gresley, *The American Conflict*, O.D. Case, 1867, p.241.

19 Parton, 1864, pp.491.

20 Ibid, p.112.

21 Ibid.

22 James Mckaye, *The Mastership and its Fruits: The emancipated slave face to face with His old master*. Loyal Publication Society, 1864, p.17. The belief in the liberation stressed by Mr. Moore was a vision of every person of African descent in the United States. Those who were in the war field as well as those who remained at home believed in the divine power to liberate them from bondage. In Thomas Wentworth Higginson's book, *Army Life in the Black Regiment*, published in 1870, there are many religious songs composed by African Americans which indicate their firm desire for the end of slavery.

23 Edward McPherson, *The Political History of the United States of America*, during the Great Rebellion from November 6, 1860, to July 4, 1864, Philp & Solomons, 1865, p.279. For the first open policy of the employment of African American see the Second Confiscation and Militia Act of July 17, 1862, In the National Archives, Teaching with documents; the Fight for Equal Rights: Black Soldiers in the Civil War, Preserving the legacy of the United States Colored Troops, the Second Confiscation and Militia Act of July 17, 1862 is called the First Official authorization to employ African Americans. Quotes of Mr. Seward and Mr. Wells, "On the 17th of July, the president signed the Second Confiscation Act, which provided among other things, for the emancipation of the slaves of traitors and of those of their abettors and for the employment of such freedmen in the suppression of the rebellion as the president might order and direct" For this quote, see John William Burgess, *The Civil War* and the Constitution, 1859 – 1865, vol.2, C. Scribner's Sons, 1901, pp. 85.

24 Thomas Wentworth Higginson, *Army Life in a Black Regiment*, Boston: Fields, Osgood & Co, 1870, p.273.

25 Ibid, pp.279.

26 The Emancipation Proclamation, January 1, 1863, see the National Archives & Record Administration.

27 Francis Bicknell Carpenter, *The Inner Life of Abraham Lincoln: Six months at the White House*, U of Nebraska Press, 1866, p.21 See also John Malcolm Forbes Ludlow, President Lincoln, Self – Pourtrayed, A. Strahan, 1866, p.105. Ludlow notes that "President Lincoln's proclamation was a promise made to His God and that He would to it!" President Lincoln also said that "I made a solemn vow before God, that if General Lee were driven back from Pennsylvania, I would crown the result by the declaration of freedom to the slaves." See page 105 in Ludlow's book.

28 Ibid.

29 Ibid, The suggestion of Secretary Steward to the president to postpone the proclamation of the liberation of African slaves due to the loss of some fights was an indication that public opinion was taken into account before making such a major decision. That means the outcome of the war was seriously measured by the cabinet of the president. With some wins, the proclamation would be welcomed by the public. On the other hand, losses in the war were counter-productive for the proclamation.

30 Moorfield Storey, *Charles Sumner,* Houghton, Miffin and Company, 1900, p.205.

31 Brown, 1867, p.120.

32 Isaac Newton Arnold, *The History of Abraham Lincoln, and the Overthrow of Slavery*, Clarke & Co, 1866, p.272. Senator Pomeroy of Kansas advocated the enlistment of African Americans in the military to suppress the rebellion in 1861 before the military emancipation of President Lincoln.

33 See quote of Hon. Thaddeus Steven on the enlistment of African Americans in the military in 1861 in the books of Samuel Walter McCall, Thaddeus Stevens, vol.32, Houghton, Mifflin, 1899, p.212.

34 Ibid, p.216.

35 See the declaration of the Colored Men's meeting in Boston in 1861 hoping to be allowed to the join the military for the suppression of the rebellion. The request was turned down by the governor because he did not have the power to do so. The information was collected from the William Wells Brown's book, *The Negro in the American Rebellion*, 1867, pp.54 – 55.

36 Greeley, 1866, p.526. See the trip of Adjutant – General Lorenzo advocating the recruitment of African Americans in southern states after the Emancipation Proclamation. Adjutant General Lorenzo went to the South to enforce the new recruiting policy of enlisting of colored soldiers.

37 Ibid, p.526 The Bureau of African military Affairs located in Washington, D.C., was organized to keep a record of all the services of African American personnel. General Silas Casey, one of the Board members, was the president. For better efficiency, a strict policy of examining candidates for commissions in the black regiments was set forth. The bureau also ordered the establishment of many stations for the recruitment of black soldiers.

38 Horace White, *Life of Lynman Trumbull*, Houghton Mifflin,1913, p.257.

39 Lyman Trumbull'ss Speech to Hon. Lyman Trumbull of Illinois on the Freedmen's Bureau – Veto Message: delivered in the Senate of the United States, February 20, 1866, Chronicle Book and Job Print, 1866, p.4.

40 For the counties of Louisiana where African Americans were not liberated by the proclamation of President Lincoln, see William Wells Brown, *The Negro in the American Rebellion*, Lee & Shepard, 1867, pp.120 – 122.

41 Parson, 1864, p.528.

42 Ibid.

43 Polk E. Johnson *A History of Kentucky and Kentuckians, The leaders of Representative Men in Commerce, Industry, and Modern Activities*, vol. 1, Lewis Publishing Company, 1912, p.376.

44 See Report of Carl Churz and Ulysee Simpson Grant. The Message of the Present of the United States. Gov. Printing Office, 1865.

45 For the condition of the South after the war and the abuses of African Americans by their former masters, see the Report of Carl Churz and Uly- see Simpson Grant, *The message of the President of the United States*, Gov. Printing Office, 1865, pp.15 – 16.

46 Alexander Tsesis, *The Thirteenth Amendment and American Freedom: A Legal History*. NYU press, 2004, p.38.

CHAPTER V

African American Law Enforcement Duties
During the War of Secession

Examining law enforcement services performed by African Americans during the American rebellion is pertinent because the investigation reveals salient data regarding the contributions made by black soldiers in peace preservation and order maintenance. African Americans made a great impact when fighting the enemies of the United States, but few scholarly researchers have examined law enforcement duties executed by men of color. Civil War authors have recorded impressive data noting how African American soldiers enforced law and order in the Confederate territory conquered by the United States. Ellis Paxson Oberholtzer, American biographer, editor, and historian; Admiral David Dixon Porter, a distinguished Civil War Navy officer, and Benjamin Quarles, African American educator, historian, scholar, and author of *The Negro in the Civil War, The Negro in the American Revolution*, and *Lincoln and the Negro* have discussed in their works law enforcement assignments entrusted to African American soldiers during the War of Seccession. In addition to the responsibilities of maintaining law and order, the aforementioned writers discuss the protection of prisoners-of-war under the African American guards. Prison regulations and procedures were recorded by prisoners-of-war and soldiers who wrote on this subject of law enforcement duties assigned to African Americans. Captain Luis Emilio, a soldier of the 54th Massachusetts Colored Infantry (first military unit of black soldiers to be raised in the North during the Civil War), recorded the prison functions of black soldiers when guarding prisoners-of-war.[1] Moreover, the authors address the relationship between prisoners and African American guards. Robert Alonzo Brock collected prison data regarding the relationship between the prisoners and African Americans employed as guards. Brock's research indicates that former slaves were assigned guard duties in the "pen" where Confederate prisoners-of-war were detained.[2] As former bondsmen, the guards had much respect for their former masters housed in the prison camp. It is worthwhile to note that any guard who had his master in custody referred to him as "Master."[3] While in the "pen," as noted by Brock, the relationship between African American guards and the prisoners seemed amiable. From the letter of William Hoffman, Colonel 3rd Infantry and Commissary-General of Prisoners, prisoners in Point Lookout, Maryland, were in excellent condition. In 1864, prisoners of war housed at Point Lookout prison numbered 10,947 men. These prisoners were kept by large numbers of soldiers. In one report, Colonel Hoffman cited 563 officers and 10,192 soldiers were assigned at Point Lookout. In addition to these numbers, 192 citizens were also employed at the prison. Soldiers assigned at the prison were under the control of Union Army Civil War volunteer, Colonel Alonzo G. Draper. Colonel Draper commanded the 36th U.S. Colored Infantry, comprised of the 5th New Hampshire Infantry, the 4th Rhode Island Infantry, and the 2nd Wisconsin Infantry—soldiers trained to use heavy artillery. When Draper concluded his campaign of enlisting colored soldiers, the 36th U.S. Colored Infantry had 753 men. At the Point Lookout Prison, Colonel Draper had with him 753 colored soldiers of the 36th U.S. Colored Infantry, 438 men were from New Hampshire, 320 men from Rhode Island, 119 from the 2nd Wisconsin Battery; 24 cavalry which made 1,654 men for the control of prisoners. These men were assigned to prison-guard duty at Point Lookout.[4] Colonel Draper and his men held this assignment for three months before being reassigned to combat operations in Petersburg and Richmond, Virginia, from the Fall of 1864 to the Spring of 1865—Civil War battles that were successful under his leadership.

Another report recorded a different attitude of Confederate

prisoners-of-war detained in the Point Lookout Prison. Confederate prisoners-of-war did not want to be guarded by black soldiers.
Thomas Edward Watson, Georgia politician, lawyer, and newspaper
editor noted that "Confederate prisoners planned a secret revolution
to kill black soldiers assigned as guards over the prison."[5] At Point
Lookout Prison, there was a history revealing that black sentinels fired
into a crowd of prisoners. To avoid the increase of the conflict between the guards and the prisoners, black soldiers were removed and
white soldiers were assigned to guard duties at Point Lookout Prison.[6]

Janet B. Hewett and John Ogden Murray, two other authors
steeped in intelligence concerning the Civil War, penned valuable information regarding military police and prison services executed by
black soldiers during the American rebellion. Murray and the previously mentioned Robert Alonzo Brock were prisoners-of-war during
the American conflict. These two former prisoners spoke of the conditions of the prisons according to their own experiences and observations. These two imprisoned veterans of the Civil War, left vivid
data about the regulations of the prisons as well as the design of the
prisons. Moreover, they discussed the temporary holding cells used
to keep prisoners before their transfer to different facilities. Murray,
who spent some days in a transit detention center aboard a schooner
hulk before being sent to the Union prison in Morris Island, South
Carolina, discussed this feature of the imprisonment saga.[7] His account of the Union prison at Morris Island was nearly the same as
Emilio's report, except for a few remarks on the treatment of the prisoners. Murray noted that prisoners were not well accommodated. He
said that "a black sergeant assigned them to tents, putting four men
in each small A-tent which would not comfortably hold more than
two men."[8] The 54th Massachusetts volunteer regiment was forced to
place as many prisoners as possible in tents due to the limited space at
the camp. The camp was not large enough to comfortably accommo-
date so many prisoners. Therefore, assigning four men to a small tent
was the best possible solution at that time. According to Murray, "the
prison stockade was built of long pine poles driven in the ground and
cleated together by pine boards. About the top of the high fence was

a parapet built so that the black guards might overlook their camp." Murray went on to state that "this pen enclosed about two acres of land. On the inside of the stockade fence, about ten feet from it, was stretched an inch rope."[9] Murray's description clearly confirms that the camp where the stockade was built was not very big. Therefore, it is at least understandable why prisoners were kept in such close living conditions.

Hewett, compiler of the supplement to the Official Records of the Union and Confederate Armies, had additional information on the guard services executed by African American soldiers.[10] Moreover, as the compiler of information about the War of the Rebellion, Hewett paid much attention to the law enforcement work entrusted to the black soldiers. She recorded salient points on African Americans' enforcement of the law. She noted such law enforcement duties as guarding prisoners of war, escorting prisoners, guarding camps, arresting rebels, and patrolling the camps and conquered Confederate territories.

Similarly, Thomas Edward Watson, in his publication *Watson's Magazine*, detailed prison life under the jurisdiction of African American guards. Further documentation that comments upon facts regarding the maintenance of law and order by African Americans has been recorded in the distinguished publication, *The War of the Rebellion: A Compilation of the Official Records of the Union and Confederate Armies*. The compilers were members of the U.S. War Department who collected authoritative data on military police and prison services performed by Union soldiers of both races in the Confederate states along with other data.

Before examining the employment of African Americans in law enforcement during the war of secession, it is important to clarify the context of this war. To comprehend the original context of the war, there are a few questions to ask: Was the conflict between the government of the United States and that of the Confederate States of America a civil war? If it was a civil war, were these two governments under the same regime? Similarly, were the states which seceded from the United States under the protection of the Constitution of the United

States? Did the seceded states form a government? Did they have a capital for their states as well as a president? Did they have a monetary system? The analysis of these questions will reveal whether the War of 1861 was surely a civil war. These questions are not asked to challenge the status of the war, but to assist in analyzing law enforcement duties performed by the soldiers according to the original context of the war.

The perception of historians with respect to the Civil War conflicts with Jefferson Davis's perspective, who was president of the Confederate States of America from 1861-1865 is not the same. He believed that the conflict between the Union and Confederate Armies was not a civil war. From his view, it was a war fought between two separate nations. President Davis viewed the Confederate States of America as an independent country with its own government officials. To illustrate this, when Davis complained about the difficulties the confederacy faced to arm soldiers, he noted that "the first difficulty that confronted the Confederate Government was how to supply army and munitions of war for men eager to defend their country. There were many more than we could arm."[11] In this statement, the president was proud to call the territory which seceded from the United States a country.

Similarly, the framing of a constitution was a move that persuaded President Davis and others to regard seceded states as having formed a country separate from the United States.[12] From this perspective, the conflict between the United States and the Confederates was not a rebellion. It was a war fought for specific causes. The United States government fought the war to preserve the Union, thus reclaiming the territory that had seceded from the Union. On the contrary, the Confederate States of America engaged in war against the United States to suppress the invasion from the Union. High ranking officials in the Confederate government stressed that they had legal rights to separate from the Union because it was within their constitutional rights. According to Confederate officials, the Constitution of the United States did not have any clauses prohibiting any state to secede from the compact formed voluntarily. Another argument which supported the existence of the Confederate government was the formal writing of a constitution for the states to observe. The seventh article of the constitution addressed the phases of its governance—the legislative branch, the executive branch, the judiciary branch, the states, amendments, the confederacy, and ratification. In addition to the constitution, the formation of a de facto government convinced some that the Confederate States of America was a country, even though civilized nations did not recognize the seceded states as a country. Like other nations, supporters of the Union as well as Union government officials rejected any recognition of the Confederate States of America as an entity to be acknowledged as a country. In regard to the government composition of the Confederate States of America, President Davis appointed cabinet members: Robert Toombs of Georgia, Secretary of State; Christopher Memminger of South Carolina, Secretary of the Treasury; LeRoy Pope Walker of Alabama, Secretary of War; Judah P. Benjamin of Louisiana, Attorney General; Stephen Mallory of Florida, Secretary of Navy, and John H. Reagan of Texas, Postmaster General. Thus, the aforementioned indicate the formation of a de facto government for a Confederate country.[13]

Regarding the Union, President Abraham Lincoln did not acknowledge the states that seceded from the Union. For this reason, he internationalized the Civil War by involving Francis Lieber, a German-American international law expert to frame the *Instructions for the Government of Armies of the United States in the Field*.[14] Lieber's instructions were the first international codification of the articles of war of the United States. In other words, Lieber's instructions outlined the rules of warfare between nations. According to Lieber, the Union invoked the Law of Nations, that is, rules and regulations governing international relations during times of war and peace, before executing the war. To illustrate, Article 67 of the *Instructions for the Government of Armies of the United States in the Field* stipulated that "the *Law of Nations* allows every sovereign government to make war upon another state and therefore, admits of no rule or law different from those of regular warfare, regarding the treatment of prisoners of war, although they may belong to the army of a government which the captor may consider as a wanton and unjust assailant."[15] Though

Lincoln did not acknowledge the cessation of states at first, his expo-sure to the *Law of Nations* shows that he came to understand that the states which seceded from the United States were no longer under the obligations of his jurisdiction and country. The seceded states had organized themselves into another entity, and, in consequence, had become another country. Therefore, those captured during the war were qualified to bear the status of prisoners-of-war.

General Benjamin Butler invoked the internationalization of war for the liberation of slaves in Virginia. When he freed the slaves who crossed the Union line, he employed the term "contraband" in ref-erence to them as justification to avoid returning the slaves to the enemy. When Major John L. Carey visited General Butler claiming the restitution of slaves protected behind Union lines for his friend Colonel Adam Gale Malloy, Butler responded to him, "I am under no constitutional obligation to a foreign country, which Virginia now claims to be."[16] This assertion indicates that the General understood the international context of the war. From his perspective, the United States was at war against a foreign nation. Therefore, Virginia, under the auspices of the secession, was regarded under constitutional law by Butler as belonging to a foreign nation.

After the Union occupied the Confederate states, the statehood claim started to diminish. Therefore, the conflict between the North and South was reduced to a state of a civil war—a conflict between members of the same country. Civilians in the occupied territories were no longer considered the enemies of the United States as in the beginning of the war. As the spirit of belonging to the United States prevailed within the Confederate states, the attachment to the Union increased progressively. Therefore, members of the Confederate states had difficulties claiming the existence of Confederate States of Amer-ica. The desertion of many soldiers from the cause of the Confederate government was another dynamic that made the claim of statehood difficult. As the claim for statehood of the Confederacy failed, the war became merely a civil war.

With the reduction of the intensity and magnitude of the Ameri-can conflict regarding statehood, the Union Army turned its attention to protecting civilians from the crimes born out of war. Thus, the Union assigned personnel to protect civilians from the violence and hostility of military bandits, deserters, and confederate guerillas. In towns, counties, and villages occupied by the Union, the Confederate civil government was no longer legitimate. Union soldiers were empowered with civilian administration of justice and law enforcement duties. Moreover, Union soldiers were prone to engage in emergency services and social services for the welfare of their countrymen. Refugees and contraband escaping from war zones to the Union lines received genuine support from the generals and federal authorities. Because the Union soldiers were perceived as protectors, many southerners assisted the northern soldiers with needed information. The information provided by the escapees influenced the decision-making of the Union in its execution of the war. For example, to some extent the information received influenced how the soldiers secured the occupied territories. On the contrary, persons who held solid convictions in favor of Confederate causes maintained their volatile attitude toward the Union. They continued to harass Union military personnel, including African Americans who supported the northern states.

In brief, the military conflict of 1861 was between a sovereign country and a country-to-be. The war and the maintenance of peace were executed in accordance to the Law of Nations. However, the continuation of the conflict reduced the fractured United States to a civil war since the dream of establishing a country was diminishing daily among Confederate officials. As a result, Union officials treated the inhabitants of the occupied Confederate states as Americans. When Union soldiers occupied the territory belonging to the Confederate government, most southerners had the same rights and immunity as the northerners in the Union states. This rule of thumb had one exception—persons who were sympathizers of Confederate causes.

After examining the dual status of the American conflict, it is feasible to examine law enforcement duties performed by African American soldiers during the rebellion. During the war between the United States and the Confederate country-to-be, African Americans were among the soldiers who defended liberty and fought on the Union side of the internal conflict. Men of color were employed as volunteer-citizen soldiers in the service of the United States. The first recruitment of African Americans in the services of the United States was conducted by General Rufus Saxton in Beaufort, South Carolina.[17] Before the arming of blacks in South Carolina, General Benjamin Butler received escaped African Americans in Virginia. He called the escapees "contraband" of war.[18] While in Virginia under the protection of General Butler, African Americans did not carry arms, but did menial work for the army. Black men started carrying arms in South Carolina under the command of General David Hunter in 1862. The history of the regiment of General Hunter started in Hilton Head, South Carolina. Susie King Taylor, the first black Army nurse and the medical practitioner for the all-black Army troops known as the 1st South Carolina Volunteers (later designated as the 33rd United States Colored Infantry Regiment), contends, "General David Hunter was the first man to arm the black man in 1862. He had a hard struggle to hold all the southern division with few men, so he applied to Congress, but the answer to him was, 'do not bother us' which was very discouraging."[19] General Hunter was in a difficult position at the time because the public was against arming black soldiers. Being a loyal Union general, he decided to form two companies of African Americans for the protection of the islands off the coast of South Carolina. including performing garrison duty.[20] From the letter written May 6, 1862, by H. W. Benham, Brigadier General to Esquire Jules De La Croix, U.S. agent in charge of contrabands, General Hunter was authorized by the War Department to fulfill his idea to organize squads and companies that he would form out of a regiment of runaway blacks who had entered the Union lines.[21] Similarly, in a letter written May 8, 1862 by Major General David Hunter, affirmed to General Isaac I. Stevens, that the War Department had given Hunter permission to form into squads or companies or perhaps into regiments a portion of black people who had escaped bondage and come across Union lines.[22] These letters show that General Hunter had the support of the War Department to organize African American regiments.

Before the official recruitment of blacks into the services of the

United States, General Hunter enforced his proclamation which liberated slaves in Georgia, Florida, and South Carolina from bondage because their masters took arms against the United States.[23] After freeing the African slaves, he enlisted them in his companies. To fulfill his regiment's purpose, General Hunter assigned James Cashman, an African American, as a military recruiter. Cashman was permitted to enlist 100 men in Ladies and Saint Helena Islands. According to Edward L. Pierce, special agent to the Treasury Department, Cashman enrolled 25-50 blacks from the Islands.[24] Pierce was connected to the abolitionists. According to Laura Joseph Webster, "[Pierce] was a young abolitionist of Boston who had formerly studied in [Salmon P.] Chase's Law Office and had superintended the labor of the 'Contrabands' at Fortress Monroe the preceding summer."[25] Apparently, Cashman was the first black employed to enforce the military enrollment under General Hunter in the South. Among Union military officers, Sergeant Charles Tyler Trowbridge, white abolitionist and politician, was in charge of the recruitment and the formation of Hunter's black regiment. President Abraham Lincoln revoked General Hunter's decision to organize a regiment comprised of runaway slaves. Lincoln noted that the general did not have the power to free black people from slavery. The revocation of Hunter's proclamation shows that the purpose of the war for President Lincoln was not the liberation of African Americans, but the preservation of the Union as he still claimed. General Hunter discontinued arming African Americans when Lincoln disapproved of the general's idea for strengthening it.

When the regiment of General Hunter was disbanded, Sergeant Trowbridge carried a group of African American soldiers to Simon's Island. Unlike in Hilton Head, South Carolina, in Kansas, an African American regiment was formed in 1862 by Colonel James Williams.[26] In fact, the Kansas black regiment was the first to be formed in the South, but the regiment was not mustered in the service of the United States. In 1862, General Thomas Wentworth Higginson took a group of slaves to form a black regiment which he commanded. The First Volunteer Colored Regiment of South Carolina was the first black regiment mustered in the services of the United States during the late

Civil War, except a portion of the troops raised by Major General Butler at New Orleans."[27] In Louisiana, General Hunter in the same year formed the "Louisiana Native Guard" with the assistance of influential black leaders of the city of New Orleans. Volunteer soldiers in the Louisiana Native Guard were educated and self-reliant. Conversely, soldiers enlisted in South Carolina for the regiment of General Thomas Wentworth Higginson were slaves and were not educated.

The Louisiana Native Guard was first formed by Governor Thomas Overton Moore, the Confederate official who mandated uneducated slaves to perform law enforcement duties. Governor Moore assigned officers of the Louisiana Native Guard with the protection of the city and its borders and forts. But after Louisiana fell to the Union, General Hunter changed his plans. After consultations and discussions with the African American leaders of New Orleans, an agreement was concluded for the formation of the Louisiana Native Guard to operate under the Union flag. Therefore, the former black Confederate soldiers were finally devoted to the defense and the preservation of the Union.

Many government officials desired and advocated enlisting black people in the United States Army. In 1862, Governor John A. Andrew gained permission from Ohio-born Edwin McMasters Stanton, the Secretary of War, to order the formation of the 54th Massachusetts black regiment.[28] He was among the first government officials in Massachusetts to be informed about the possible military confrontation between the South and the Union. General Benjamin Butler advised Stanton to get the Massachusetts militia ready, anticipating the war of the secession. Senator Henry Wilson of Massachusetts, a strong opponent of slavery, was also aware of Butler's information on the preparation of war by the southerners. They were determined to be prepared for internal warfare.[29] From 1863 to 1864, many states in the Union were authorized to form regiments of black soldiers. The government of the United States dispatched General Lorenzo Thomas to the Mississippi valley to initiate and supervise the recruitment of black regiments. Thomas went to Tennessee for the same purpose. The War Department established recruiting stations in Maryland, Missouri, and Tennessee to enlist able-bodied, free African Americans.[30] John Stevens Cabot Abbott, a 19th century historian and biographer wrote that "a number of black regiments were organized in the Western Department, by orders of the General Government and under the direct supervision of Adjutant-General Thomas."[31] In 1864, the First Regiment, Tennessee Heavy Artillery (African descent) was formed in Knoxville.[32] This black force was involved in law enforcement, unlike the 54th Massachusetts Infantry whose primary responsibility was to guard prisoners-of-war. The 12th Regiment, United States Colored Infantry; 13th Regiment United States Infantry, and the 15th Regiment, United States Colored Infantry, were assigned law enforcement duties guarding government properties. In like manner, the 1st Louisiana Native Guard, one of the first all-black regiments to fight in the Union Army, was entrusted with law enforcement duties along with other black forces. They also performed guard and escort duties during the civil war conflict.

In 1863, the 54th regiment of the Massachusetts Volunteer Infantry operated under the command of Robert Gould Shaw, member of a prominent abolitionist Boston family. Gould has been credited with being attached to the causes of people of the African race, a passion he inherited from his father, Francis George Shaw, a social reformer and staunch abolitionist.[33] Major Robert Gould Shaw was killed at Fort Wagner, a beachhead near Charleston, South Carolina while leading his men to the enemy fort. Shaw was succeeded by Colonel James Montgomery whom Luis F. Emilio described as a noble man. Montgomery was the first high-ranking officer who received contraband slaves in Virginia when he was under the command of General Butler.

The Massachusetts black regiment soldiers were recruited and assembled by many recruiting officers. Among these officers were abolitionists such as Frederick Douglass, a former slave, social reformer, author, and statesman; John Mercer Langston, an educator, attorney, and the first African American to hold elected office in the United States; and black church leaders in Boston, Massachusetts. Some government leaders in Boston were also engaged in the recruitment of the Massachusetts black regiments. Governor John A. Andrew was the architect of the Massachusetts black regiment. From the beginning of the war, he advocated for the enlistment of black soldiers to suppress the rebellion.

At the start of the growing separation between the North and South, the soldiers in African American regiments were not paid. They assumed patriotic duties for the country possibly hoping to be liberated after the war if the Union succeeded in taking control of southern territories. It was in 1863 that the United States decided to pay black soldiers half of the salary white soldiers were paid. However, African American soldiers refused to accept partial salary because they expected to receive full pay. Susie King Taylor noted that when black soldiers rejected the offer of half pay, they preferred to give their services to the government voluntarily, which they did until 1864 when the government granted them full salary, including retroactive pay.[34] The equal pay for African American soldiers during the Civil War was advocated by many people including Frederick Douglass. With the assistance of government officials, Douglass was introduced to President Lincoln and the Secretary of War Edwin Stanton, to speak about the pay of the black soldiers. Massachusetts Senator Charles Sumner, Kansas Senator Samuel Pomeroy, and Massachusetts Senator Henry Wilson were government officials who worked cordially with Douglass in his fight concerning equal pay to military men serving in the U.S. Army. Upon Douglass' arrival in Washington, D.C., to see President Lincoln, the president told him that he knew his concern about equal pay for both white and black soldiers.[35] In addition to the topic of equal pay, Douglass discussed further concerns about African Americans who had been taken prisoners-of-war by the Confederate soldiers and had either been enslaved or sold into slavery.

In regard to the maintenance of peace and order during the Civil War, the role of African Americans was unlike their roles during the War of 1812. In their participation in the Civil War, African Americans performed law enforcement duties in many Southern cities. Black soldiers were authorized to execute police duties, prison duties, and security services throughout the many camps, settlements, and towns in the occupied Confederate regions.

Law Enforcement Services Performed
by African American Soldiers

Law enforcement services during war time are as critical for the success of the war as battles in the field. No army can win a war without securing the conquered territory. In our modern era, the Iraq War is a palpable example that when military police duties are overlooked, the efforts made during the fighting seem to be lost. When law enforcement duties are taken less seriously, the enemies travel freely in the conquered territory and conduct without constraint guerrilla warfare against the conqueror's army. But during the War of Secession, Union generals anticipated the attacks of the Confederate soldiers. Therefore, military policing was well planned to overcome any attacks from the enemy. Various documents explored revealed that the duties performed by Union military police were valuable for the protection of people and property in the conquered lands.[36] Union military police played an important role in their contribution to the success of the war between the United States and the Confederate States of America. In many cities under the occupation of the federal government, Confederate soldiers were prevented from rendering the territories ungovernable. Government properties were well guarded, and precautions were taken to protect lines of communications such as trains, railroads, and telegraphs. Similarly, weapon depots were guarded to avoid being destroyed by Confederate soldiers. Furthermore, a mechanism was put in place for the exchange process for prisoners-of-war. Without well-orchestrated law enforcement strategies, soldiers in the war zones would be at a great disadvantage fighting a war and, simultaneously, attempting to preserve the peace in the conquered land. Union generals selected cavalry and infantry regiments for the performance of law enforcement duties. The work of Janet B. Hewett, *The Roster of Union Soldiers, 1861-1865,* confirms that the Union Army assigned soldiers whose specific command was to enforce the law. She lists the 1st United States Colored Cavalry, the 3rd United States Cavalry, the 5th Massachusetts Colored Cavalry, the 4th United States Colored Heavy Artillery, the 9th United State Colored Infantry, the 10th United States Colored Infantry, the 11th United States Colored

Infantry, the 17th United States Colored Infantry, the 18th United States Colored Infantry, and the 26th Colored Infantry as troops who were assigned with regular law enforcement duties.[37] In addition to the listed cavalry and infantry, other regiments and cavalry performed law enforcement duties such as the 54th and 55th Massachusetts black regiments. Similarly, regiments formed of white soldiers were also entrusted with law enforcement duties in regions where African Americans were not entrusted with military police duties, such as in Nashville, Tennessee. In Nashville, the Confederate spirit was high, so it was not a congenial move to engage African Americans in police work. Such a decision would infuriate many confederate sympathizers and create problems.

The history of military police in the United States can be traced back to the Colonial Era. During war time and when Native Americans attacked settlements, colonial officials ordered militiamen to scout around towns and in areas where the enemy was expected to attack. Militia scouting worked along with patrol duties. During the Revolutionary War of 1775, the generals were protected by body servants. These body servants were actually guards who provided security for the generals. To illustrate, General William Whipple of the New Hampshire militia during the Revolutionary War had an African American manservant, Prince Whipple. The protection of the generals usually was under the care of a manservant. However, in 1776, the Commander in Chief, General George Washington's security was assigned to guards.[38] The general's guards were sometimes called the commander in chief's guards. In 1778, a small squad of cavalrymen were from time-to-time assigned to the escort duties of General Washington.[39] In the same year, a captain was given the responsibilities of a provost, or an administrative officer. The captain convened four lieutenants, one clerk, a quarter–master sergeant, two trumpeters, two sergeants, five corporals, and forty-three privates to assign them the task to apprehend deserters, rioters, and smugglers.[40] These officers, performing provost guards, were responsible for maintaining physical locations of the Union. It was also during the Revolutionary War that the provost marshal was given law enforcement and judiciary duties. Captain Barttholomew Von Heer was the provost marshal of the Continental Army.[41]

During the war between the United States and the de facto Confederate country, the Provost Marshal Department at the Potomac was under Colonel Andrew Porter of the 16th Infantry Regiment. He was a provost marshal of Washington, D.C., Porter's law enforcement duties included the suppression of depredations and disturbances and the preservation of good order beyond the limits of the camp. In addition, he suppressed vices such as operating gambling houses, drinking houses, bar-rooms, and brothels that were under his jurisdiction. Moreover, he was entrusted with the regulatory power of hotels, taverns, markets, and places of public amusement.[42] The provost marshal had the power to search, seize, arrest, and execute sentences of general court–martials including imprisonment in cases that resulted in capital punishment. The enforcement of the sale of intoxicating liquors was also under his court's jurisdiction.[43] In the same division, soldiers were empowered with provost guard duties. Among African Americans, Captain Luis Emilio of the 54th Massachusetts black regiment appears as acting assistant provost marshal of the division.[44] Possibly with the title of acting assistant provost marshal, he had the power to adjudicate cases in his division. In like manner, he more than likely punished soldiers who disobeyed military rules.

Like in the Revolutionary War, during the War of Secession military police activities were performed regularly. Generals from various regiments selected companies which were assigned for the maintenance of peace and order in the conquered territories. As for African Americans, it was on August 25, 1862, that the War Department in Washington, D.C., authorized black soldiers to perform law enforcement duties. According to General Thomas Wentworth Higginson, the War Department ordered "the organization in any convenient squads, companies, battalions, regiments, and brigades for a number not exceeding fifty thousand and muster them into the service of the United States for the term of the war."[45] "The soldiers were ordered to guard the plantations and settlements occupied by the United States from invasion, and protect the inhabitants thereof from captivity and murder by the enemies."[46] For the execution of the military police, the Secretary of War ordered that "they be armed, uniformed, and equipped."[47] Apparently, the order by the secretary of war was the first of this kind to order the performance of the military police by African American volunteer soldiers. From this order, African Americans were legally empowered by the authorities of the federal government to enforce the rules, regulations, and laws imposed by the soldiers in the controlled areas.

The narrative of law enforcement services of white and black soldiers during the Civil War was not fully explored for many years after the war. Historians who have covered the War of Secession have focused more on the fighting abilities of black soldiers and their white brethren in arms, but their law enforcement duties is less explored. Historians have put much weight on the outcome of the fighting abilities of both races, but minuscule attention has been given to the maintenance of law and order in the conquered territories. Even though there is little focus on the military police duties executed during the war, many military men, historians, and scholars have recorded abundant material that discusses and explains the military tactics used by Union soldiers to secure towns, villages, and settlements once these territories came under Union jurisdiction. In addition, police services conducted by military officers in the former Confederate states have been noted. Authors such as Thomas Wentworth Higginson, William A. Dobak, William Wells Brown, Benjamin Quarles, Luis Fenollosa Emilio, Janet B. Hewett, Phineas Camp Headley, John Towsend Trowbridge, and Whitelaw Reid, have documented the performance of law enforcement duties by black soldiers. However, this work goes beyond just documenting that black soldiers existed in the military as law enforcers; this pieces together the role played by black soldiers in the maintenance of peace and order in the occupied territories of the Confederate de facto republic. In addition, this book details the prison services assumed by African American soldiers, documents the security African American men provided Union military generals and also discusses the dfferences made in the assigned military police duties performed by African Americans and their white brethren in arms in territories where African Americans were denied the power to enforce the law. In these areas white soldiers were entrusted with all law enforcement duties. In the state of Tennessee, only white soldiers could enforce the law. Similarly, in the towns and villages under the jurisdiction of those who were loyal to the Union, African Americans were excluded from any law enforcement duties which would physically put them in contact with white inhabitants. During the time when the Civil War was executed, African Americans were not admitted in many geographical areas in the South as equal to their white counterparts. Therefore, authorizing black men to patrol in such zones would be comparable to putting a torch to a keg of gun powder—resulting in a massive explosion.

During the war, at any given time, military officers or militiamen were assigned military police duties to detect and control crime, apprehend criminals, arrest criminals, detain suspected criminals, and guard prisoners. The officers also performed social and emergency services for people in distress. Unlike in the modern era, during the War of Secession African American soldiers and militiamen were entrusted with various law enforcement duties. According to the documents consulted, Union soldiers were empowered with various law enforcement duties in the occupied territories. Unlike other Union military officers, black soldiers patrolled the camps, freedmen settlements and towns, made arrests, guarded government and private properties, guarded prisoners-of-war, controlled crimes, and performed social and emergency services. To illustrate, in the black regiment of General Thomas Wentworth Higginson, Sergeant Prince Rivers, an escaped slave from Beaufort, South Carolina who became a soldier in the Union Army, had the entire charge of the prisoners and the daily policing of the camp. Sergeant Rivers, who later became Captain Rivers, was a man of distinguished appearance. Before escaping to the Union Army, he served with the household staff, and he was a former coachman on the Oak Point Plantation in Beaufort owned by Henry Middleton Stuart, Sr. Rivers was also a sergeant in the old regiment of General David Hunter.[48] Captain Rivers was a very capable man, He had the power to control his fellow soldiers. Because of his writing skills, Rivers was able to report the daily camp activities. In the opinion of Colonel Higginson, if there should ever be a black monarchy in South Carolina, Rivers would be its king.[49]

Another example of outstanding military leadership among black soldiers is noted in the duties of Corporal Prince Lambkin, one of the black guards and an able man. Lambkin once made an inspiring speech in camp to his fellow African Americans. He told them they lived under the flag of the United States and would die for it.[50] Moreover, Corporal Robert Sutton was charged with piloting a ship on the St. Mary's River. Piloting is the same as patrolling on the water highway. He was the wisest man among those in his rank, and he was meditative and a systematic intellect.[51] These are only a few illustrations of law enforcement duties performed by African Americans at the beginning of the war.

As early as 1861, Robert Smalls, while still a slave, commandeered the *USS Planter*, a Confederate warship, and escaped with the ship to the Union camp. For his loyalty and patriotism to the Union, he was appointed a pilot in the United States Navy after dispatching the *Planter* to the Union camp. David Dixon Porter, U. S. Navy admiral and Medal of Honor recipient, identified Smalls as "a very clever light mulatto."[52] Porter went on to state that "he [Smalls] gave valuable information which only a man of his intelligence could import. Smalls was also patrolling the water highway during his employment with the Union."[53] With respect to law enforcement duties performed by black soldiers, their eclectic assignments included patrolling services, doing emergency services, making arrests, escorting, and guarding prisoners and government properties.

Patrol Services

Patroling is one of the public's most valued services among law enforcement functions. Unlike in peace time, during wartime soldiers have to maintain law and order in the areas under their occupation. In addition, the lines of communication are protected by military men. While in time of peace these services are performed by police officers, in time of war, military police are empowered with the duties that are usually relegated to civilian police. In 1861, when southern state government officials formed a de facto government, they were no longer under the obligations to observe the laws of the United States. Moreover, the Constitution of the United States did not have any legal effect on inhabitants of the Confederate States of America. Neither were these states under the protection of the Constitution of the United States. Government officials and their inhabitants were therefore regarded as enemies of the United States. By declaring war against the U.S. government, the seceded confederacy was obligated to recuperate the territories they believed belonged to them. Therefore, the United States government was obligated to use force to protect the Union from balkanization. As a consequence, these states were treated as conquered land upon occupation and subjected to military rule under the flag of the United States. As a result, law and order was maintained by the soldiers. On the contrary, the Confederate's government officials treated Union soldiers as invaders in their territory. They were compelled to employ guerillas tactics to regain the control of the conquered land. But the American generals were well prepared to protect civilians and properties in the occupied territories. Military police assigned with law enforcement duties were selected by the generals. Soldiers entrusted with the maintenance of peace and order differed from town to town and settlement to settlement. For example, in the city of Nashville, African Americans were not permitted to conduct patrol services possibly avoiding infuriating Union supports. Law and order was maintained by the white soldiers from Ohio. On the contrary, in South Carolina, Mississippi, Louisiana, and Alabama where African Americans were numerous and the spirit of the Confederate was strong, the generals were pleased to empower black soldiers with patrol services. In Nashville, African American soldiers performed other law enforcement duties such as guarding bridges and railroad trains. Similarly, in Louisiana, in the areas under Union control, African Americans were not given patrol duties. In these areas, they were still property of their masters as the proclamation of President Lincoln stressed.

Patrol services in the South were dangerous and risky because Confederate soldiers counducted guerilla warfare whenever they pleased. They were under pressure to keep the land which they held. The dangerousness of patrol duties in the South was expressed by Ellis Paxson Oberholtzer. According to him "the unpleasant task of policing the south could be left to the blacks who were accustomed to the climate."[54] This indicates that other soldiers disliked performing police work which they believed was dangerous to their safety. During the war and thereafter, Union soldiers protected African Americans and white people who were loyal to them. It appears that African Americans needed the Union's protection more than other subjects. Therefore, as the duty of policing was unpleasant to other soldiers, black soldiers were obligated to protect and defend their brethren in most cases. This was measurable in South Carolina, Mississippi, Alabama, and Louisiana where the population of African Americans was large.

From 1862 to 1865 black soldiers performed law enforcement duties in many cities and camps. As for patrol services, as we mentioned earlier, we found that African Americans performed patrol services in the camp under the jurisdiction of General Thomas Wentworth Higginson in 1862. At this camp, Sergeant Prince Rivers, a black man, was ordered to conduct daily patrol of the camp to deter enemies from committing evil acts to Union soldiers.[55] In the same year, in Louisiana, soldiers in Company K, 74th United States Colored Infantry (formally 2nd Regiment, Louisiana Native Guard and 2nd Regiment Infantry, Corps d'Afrique) were assigned to maintain peace and order in the towns surrounding the post at the Headquarter at the Boute Station.[56] This mission was entrusted to soldiers of Company K patrol and it was important for the security of the surrounding areas of the Boute Stations. They deterred guerrillas who attempted to attack civilians and soldiers. Possibly, at the Boute Station and the surrounding areas, there were many people loyal to the Union. In addition, to the maintenance of peace and order, this company also performed guard duties in the same areas where they were entrusted with the restoration of peace and order. In 1862, due to the magnitude of the confrontation, it is plausible to stipulate that the 1st South Carolina regiment, the Louisiana Native Guard, the First Kansas Colored regiment, and the 54th Massachusetts were entrusted with police work.

In 1863, after the military necessity of President Lincoln's Emancipation Proclamation, many African American military regiments were formed. With the increase of the number of black regiments, there was an increased employment of African American soldiers in law enforcement. In cities such as Memphis, African American soldiers were engaged in law and order maintenance from 1863 to when they were mustered out of the service of the United States. In 1863, Company G of the 3rd United States Colored Cavalry (formally the First Mississippi Cavalry, Corps d'Afrique) was engaged in patrolling the surrounding areas near Memphis where they were stationed.[57] The Congressional record on the Memphis riots of 1866 notes that "the 3rd Regiment of United States Colored Artillery which stationed at Memphis from the time of its organization had been employed in various police duties that brought it members into frequent contact with the lawless white element."[58] This statement shows that law and order in Memphis was maintained by the black soldiers from the period of 1863 to 1866, when they were mustered out of the service of the United States. It appears that the 3rd regiment of the United States Colored Artillery was one of the longest lasting forces of black soldiers employed in the military police in a big city. Police duties performed by African American soldiers were credited by many generals. General Stoneman's testimony on the African American soldiers was as follows: "I must say, in justice to the colored troops, that their conduct compared very favorable, with that of the same number of the white troops under similar circumstance."[59] The general was impartial while giving his testimony. He spoke about the conduct of the black soldiers according to the events which he witnessed. Major General Stoneman was the commanding officer of the Department of Tennessee which was headquartered in Memphis. Similarly, Lieutenant Garrett and Hastings noted that "whenever it became necessary for the black soldiers to make arrest of white citizens, it was done in an orderly and proper manner."[60] It looks like black soldiers acted professionally while performing police duties. Contrary to the account of the generals, from the report of the Committees of the House of Representatives on the Memphis riots, we discovered that black soldiers and Irish subjects were at odds. Hostility existed between the two parties. When the black soldiers were empowered with patrol services, they were often in contact with the Irish police. The report also revealed that when the Irish police arrested a black person, the arrests were sometimes frivolous or sometimes without cause and were made in a brutal manner. They were also sometimes beaten until being knocked down.[61] But when black people arrested white people, there were no disposition on their part to mistreat white people or attack them as noted by Lieutenant Garrett and Hastings as well as other officers.[62]

Near the city of Memphis, the Union established Camp Pickering where colored soldiers resided with their families. According to John McLeod Keating and O.F. Vedder (1888), 4,000 African American troops were stationed at Camp Pickering.[63] Some of these African Americans escaped from the enemies and sought protection from the federal government. Fearing attacks from enemies, Union officers were compelled to empower African American soldiers with patrol services to deter enemies. Possibly, enemies conducted guerillas warfare in that region against supporters of the federal government, including freedmen. The service was also important for the protection of slaves from their masters who attempted to recuperate them from the custody of the Union. In this city, the contraband slaves who escaped from various plantations sought refuge in the Union lines. Therefore, the soldiers ensured their security. Similar to Memphis, in East Tennessee, African American soldiers were also assigned military police duties. Walter T. Durham recorded that African American soldiers were mocked while guarding the outside of the city.[64]

In 1863, according to the letter written at the Headquarters Department of Tennessee near Vicksburg in July 1863, an all black male collective was organized into various parties with the purpose of policing the ground around the city.[65] Due to the large geographical areas covered by Union soldiers in the South, it is difficult to know the exact number of towns where African Americans performed police duties.

In 1864, Company I of the 50th United States Colored Infantry, which was stationed at Vicksburg, Mississippi from November to December 1864 was entrusted with patrolling the city for two months.[66] The performance of patrol duties by military police in Vicksburg, Mississippi was critical for the protection of people and property, including the success of the Union for further occupations of other cities on the Mississippi River. Geographically, the city of Vicksburg was important for the execution of the war by the Union and the Confederates. Rear-Admiral Porter noted that "the fall of Vicksburg ensured the fall of port Hudson and the opening of the Mississippi River."[67] The statement of Admiral Porter reveals the reason why colored soldiers were empowered with patrol and scouting duties around Vicksburg. It appears that the Confederate soldiers were determined to reoccupy the city. Therefore, an aggressive patrol was needed to deter them from victimizing people as well as destroying Union properties.

Like the 50th United States Colored Infantry, the 9th United States Colored Infantry which was stationed at Hilton Head, South Carolina, conducted patrol services in that city. In Hilton Head, there were many African Americans who escaped from the nearby plantations. Evert Augustus Duyckinck tells us that "in Beaufort and Hilton Head" there were about eight thousand African Americans.[68] In the city of Beaufort alone, the population of African Americans was 600. In addition, in Hilton Head, Union soldiers were stationed there and were vulnerable to the enemy's attacks. Beaufort, the town close to Hilton Head, was heavily militarized during the Civil War. Patrol duties were conducted daily to deter the enemies. Hilton Head was the first military post established in the South during the war. It was also in this city where General Hunter formed his black regiment, which has been previously discussed. African Americans who were stationed at Hilton Head were for the most part employed by the United States in many capacities such as cooks, servants, and quartermaster's employees.

In Louisiana, the 62nd United States Colored Infantry policed the camp each day at Morganza where they were stationed.[69] Patrol duties performed by colored military police continued even during the total occupation of the Confederate states. In Louisiana, the support of the Confederate government was strong. Inhabitants of that state were antagonistic to the Union's rule. In addition, they spoke up against any attempt of including African Americans in the body politic. Furthermore, violence against African Americans was rampant. Therefore, patrol services were needed for their protection.

In 1865, many capitals of the Confederate states were under the control of the Union. Unlike the capital cities, strategic towns and cities were also occupied by the Union. As an illustration, the city of Memphis was under full control of the Union in 1865. The city was close to the water highway and very important for the movement of the soldiers to different Confederate zones. Therefore, the town of Memphis was under the rule of the United States. Union soldiers were empowered with the enforcement of law and the maintenance of order. Black soldiers were also entrusted with police work before being mustered out of the United States service. From the Congressional Report we discovered that "the 1st Tennessee Heavy Artillery made up of runaway slaves performed various police and other semi-military duties."[70] In April 1865, the 3rd United States Cavalry (formerly the 1st Mississippi Cavalry, Corps d'Afrique) under Lieutenant Lorenzo Haynes also performed patrol services. According to Hewett, Company C of this regiment moved out to white's station, where it remained doing patrol and pickup duty.[71] Unlike Company C in 1865, colored soldiers of Company G in the 3rd United States Colored Cavalry patrolled the area near Memphis. This force was stationed in Memphis.[72]

On February 18, 1865, when Charleston fell into the control of the Union, colored troops as well as their white counterparts patrolled the city. According to Luis Febollosa Emilio, officer in the 54th Regiment of Massachusetts Volunteers, African American soldiers were quartered in the Cidadel. From thence they were dispatched to patrol services in the upper district of the city.[73] Similar patrol duties were performed by black soldiers in South Carolina and was mentioned by Janet B. Hewett. This author noted that "black soldiers enlisted in the 9th United States Colored Infantry stationed at Hilton Head, South Carolina, from March to April 1864 were engaged in patrol services and outpost duty on special orders from Colonel Hoyt, commanding post.[74] Colored troops also possibly policed the areas predominately inhabited by black subjects. The main object of colored soldier's patrol duties was to protect civilians from Confederate abuses. We find that the 26th United States Infantry from February to June 1865 was stationed at Pocotoligo, South Carolina, and restored and maintained law and order.

Patrol services conducted by the colored soldiers were very critical for the protection of people and properties. Loyal supporters of the Union, including African Americans, were detested by the soldiers of the Confederate armies. Towns, camps, and other settlements between the Combahee and Savannah River were not safe from the enemies. Therefore, soldiers of Company A of the 26th United States Colored Infantry remained there to maintain and restore order. Similarly, colored officers of Company B were stationed at Pocotaligo, Beach Branch, and Beaufort, South Carolina, for the maintenance of order in those areas. Soldiers of the 26th United States Colored Infantry were also stationed at Hammock, Walterborough, Grahamville, Fort Duana, Gillisonville, Robertsville, and Mcphersonville, South Carolina maintaining order. In addition, they protected whites and blacks from suffering and abuse.

Emergency Services

Emergencies services are also part of law enforcement duties. Unlike modern police and other law enforcement officers, African American soldiers assisted people in despair. When the confederate soldiers burned cities, Union generals ordered their soldiers to extinguish the fire. In Memphis for example, soldiers of Company A, the 3rd United States Colored Artillery (Heavy), provided temporary shelters to the victims of the fire. They assisted those who were scalded and had bruises more than they assisted others. This force also handed over blankets to people in distress. The 3rd United States Colored Artillery was under Lieutenant Yates at the time that they assisted the inhabitants of Memphis during emergency time.[75] Similar to Memphis, when the city of Charleston was burnt by the rebels after leaving the city, black soldiers also acted as fire fighters extinguishing fires and saving properties according to Susie King Taylor, a wife of a soldier in the 1st South Carolina Volunteer regiment and a nurse during the Civil War.[76] Susie also noted that it was a bad experience and for three or four days black soldiers were busy extinguishing fires.[77] Similarly, soldiers of the black regiment assisted distressed people. These soldiers were in the city for four to five days extinguishing fires.

Similarly, at the fall of Richmond in Virginia, African American soldiers joined their white brethren in assisting people in despair when the city was burned. Social work such as emergency assistance is also part of police assignments. When police officers help members of the community, they create a good working relationship. On the other hand, community members are happy to share information of a crime with them. In the case of black soldiers in Charleston, Taylor tells us that they were unmolested by white people due to their humane services even though they disliked them.[78] Possibly, the colored soldiers continued to perform emergency and social services in many towns and settlements where people were in distress.

Making Arrests

African American soldiers under the power of the Union were entrusted with the duties of arresting rebellious soldiers and enemy combatants during the Civil War just like white soldiers. Arresting Confederate soldiers was one of the mandates of Union military police. Soldiers performed patrol services or scouted and both African American and white soldiers arrested Confederate military men who took arms against the United States. There is plenty of documentation about the arrests of Confederate soldiers who attacked the Union lines as well as camps. The arrests of Confederate soldiers and government officials of that institution were acts of general deterrence. Such deterrence happened in Missouri when guerrilla men burnt the railroad bridge. In response, General Schofield, in command of Northern Missouri, captured the guerrilla men and subjected them to martial court. After a speedy sentence and the testimony of an African American, the guerilla leaders were shot.[78] The summary killing of the guerillas alarmed sympathizers of the Confederates. As a result, they called for the removal of General Schofield from the command of the Northern Missouri.[80] As for deterring violence, it is unknown whether or not this event had an effect on the general sympathizers of the Confederate government.

Both black and white soldiers in Union ranks arrested Confederate soldiers. John Stevens Cabot Abbot talks about a courageous and heroic black soldier who took his master prisoner during the military confrontation for the occupation of the city of Vicksburg.[81] Similar to the Confederate soldiers, government officials in the Confederate regime were also arrested when they were discovered by Union soldiers. Captain Luis Fenollosa Emilio, one the black soldiers of the 54th Regiment of the Massachusetts Volunteers recorded that during the fall of Charleston, many prominent secessionists were arrested by Union soldiers. George A. Trenholm, the Confederate Secretary of the Treasury was among Confederate officials arrested by a black regiment.[82] The power of arrest entrusted to military men in the Union continued even after the Civil War. During the military regime, under the governors appointed by the president with the consent of Congress, law and order in the former Confederate states were under the jurisdiction of military men. Similarly, other law enforcement duties during the same period were under military officers. The military governors were always the judge and law makers. They had executive and legislative powers to some extent. They appointed minor officers and enacted laws through orders.

The arrest of Confederate soldiers was one of the crime control strategies employed to discourage them from supporting a government which was against the United States. During the war, the enforcement of specific and general deterrences was necessary for the protection of Union soldiers as well as people loyal to the cause of the Union, specifically African Americans. There are plenty of documents revealing the abuse of Union soldiers by Confederate military men. Likely, Union soldiers also mistreated Confederate army men and other members of the security apparatus. During the war of rebellion, after the arrest of suspected soldiers, the suspect was always detained and escorted to the detention center for further processing. When the Civil War was fought, Union commanders established many detention centers in the camps where they were stationed. Some detention centers were also established in cities. The examination of the detentions, jail, and prisons will be conducted later in this chapter.

Escort Services by Colored Troops

Escort services by colored soldiers were performed consistently during the Civil War. While the war went on, the Union's military freights were transported by trains and warships. Like military equipment, commercial freights were also sometimes escorted by soldiers fearing an attack from Confederate soldiers as well as their followers. Moreover, prisoners were also transported by train or ship to a detention or prison. For the security of the trains, military men were selected as escorts. Among soldiers empowered with escort duties were African American troops. It seems that military police escorted trains in the routes where attacks were imminent. To illustrate, in 1864, Company G of the 62nd United States Colored Infantry, which was stationed in Natchez, Mississippi, formed an escort to a forage train going to the Reynolds' plantations for a distance of twenty four miles.[83] Similarly, the 60th United States Colored Infantry was engaged in escort duties when it was stationed at Little Rock, Arkansas, March to April 1865.[84]

With regard to the escort of prisoners, Luis Fenollosa Emilio, an African American captain in the 54th regiment of the Massachusetts Volunteer Infantry, recorded that "when colonel Hallowell with companies D, E, G, and K arrived with Confederate soldiers from landing, where the Steamer "Cossack" arrived, the escort of these prisoners of war was composed entirely of the 21st United States Colored Troops in columns, and then on either side by two companies of the 54th, the Confederates were taken to the camp."[85] The escorts of enemy combatants were conducted regularly through the Civil War to the camps, jails, or federal prisons.

Guarding Prisoners of War

During the Civil War, Union officials established many prison camps throughout the southern states. In addition to the prison camps, jails and federal prisons were also employed for the incarceration of Confederate prisoners. Similarly, in the North, facilities were also reserved for the housing of prisoners of war. At Ship Island in Mississippi, United States officials established a prison for the imprisonment of prisoners. In addition to prisons, jails were also set up in Norfolk, Virginia for the same purpose. In the state of Maryland, Point Lookout Prison was fully operational for guarding prisoners. In Morris Island, South Carolina, a prison was built for the same reasons. In 1864, 600 rebel officers were incarcerated at Morris Island. Company D of the 54th Massachusetts Colored Infantry was engaged for two months at Morris Island guarding prisoners of war.[86] In addition to the prisons, detentions were also organized for the temporary housing of prisoners of war before they were transported to the prison. John Ogden Murray talks about the "two Old Shooner Hulks" where Confederate prisoners of war were detained before being transported to the prison in Morris Island. He noted that the "Jno. A. Genet" and the "Transit," were employed as a prison. These hulks were guarded by the African American soldiers from the 54th Massachusetts Volunteer Regiment. According to Murray, the hulks were not well managed and were filled with rats and vermin.[87]

Guard services performed by African American soldiers at the federal prisons and camps have been discussed by authors who focus on the history of the Civil War and Reconstruction Period. Captain Emilio, Joseph Thomas Wilson, John Steven Cabot Abbott, and James R. Hewett have discussed black troops guarding Confederate prisoners. As early as 1862, African Americans were entrusted with the duties of guarding Confederate prisoners of war. Military officers who rebelled and engaged in military hostility against the United States lost the immunities and privileges guaranteed by the Constitution of the United States. Similarly, like the officers, individual citizens who supported the cause of the Confederate government were also treated with the same conditions. As prisoners of war, Confederate officers were protected by the Law of Nations. When Southern states revolted against the United States, the government of the United States established military laws for the management of prisoners of war. The architect of these laws was Francis Lieber. By the request of President Lincoln, he put into action laws designed for the adjudication of cases pertaining to soldiers and officials of the Confederate government arrested during the conflict.

As the states which seceded against the United States formed a de facto country, the Law of the Nations was invoked for the protection of prisoners. They [the prisoners] had the right to be protected against physical harm, the right to accommodation, the right to be liberated through an exchange process, and the right to medical treatment. In regard to the exchange process, records show that fifty Confederate officers were exchanged for the same number of black soldiers imprisoned in the Confederate correctional facilities in Charleston, South Carolina.[88] Throughout the period of the conflict, prison exchange was common.

The United States Secretary of War and General Foster entrusted Col. E.N. Hallowell, the commanding officer of the 54th Massachusetts Colored Regiment, with the management of prisoners at Morris Island. Murray writes that Col. Hallowell was charged with the administration of the prison due to his brutal nature.[89] It is unknown whether Murray's statement is factual or his own opinion. Contrary to Murray's views, R. Saxton, Brig-Gen. of the United States army wrote to General J. G. Foster in 1864 that "he believed no better officer than Colonel Hallowell can be found in whose hands to place the prisoners for their safe keeping, and thus for the duty has been well performed."[90] The account of Saxton conflicts with that of Murray in regard to the comportment of Colonel Hallowell.

Detainees were sometimes also transported to the federal prisons and jails in other cities. In some federal prisons and jails, colored soldiers were assigned as guards. For instance, at Point Lookout Prison, African American soldiers were employed as prison guards. Thomas Edward Watson writes that black soldiers were assigned for guard duties at this prison. He also discussed a plan designed by the Confederate prisoners of war to break through the stockade fence of the prison and kill every black soldier on the point.[91] Moreover, he noted that black sentinels fired upon the prisoners at the point before their arrival at the prison. Due to this incident, black soldiers were removed from guard duties at the Point Lookout Prison and white soldiers took over the assignment of guarding the prisoners of war at that facility.

In 1862, black soldiers from the 74th United States Colored Infantry (formerly the 2nd regiment, Louisiana Native Guard) were guarding prisoners at Ship Island, Mississippi. The assignments of guarding prisoners were also entrusted to companies B, G, and K of the 74th United States Colored Infantry.[92] In 1865, the Confederate prisoners incarcerated in the city jail in Norfolk, Virginia, were guarded by colored troops from the 1st United States Colored Cavalry.[93] Similarly, black soldiers stationed at Point Lookout, Maryland, were guarding prisoners of war in 1864. Company A of the 5th Massachusetts Colored Cavalry was assigned with guarding prisoners at Point Lookout, Maryland.[94] In Little Rock, Arkansas, black soldiers in Company H of the 60th United States Colored Infantry were guarding prisoners at the military prison. Some soldiers of this company were assigned with guarding prisoners in Columbus, Ohio. Afterwards, they were transferred from Little Rock, Arkansas.[95]

In the prison camp of Colonel Halowell, 560 Confederate soldiers were incarcerated. The appearances of these soldiers varied from tall and lank mountaineers to the typical southerners of the books: dark, long haired, and strong. The majority were in the poorer class of southerners. Among them, German and Irish men were included."[96] They wore suits of blue jeans and a few were in costumes of gray, more or less trimmed. Upon their heads, they wore all sorts of coverings – straw and slouch hats, and forage caps of gray, blue, or red, decorated with braid. They also wore cavalry boots, shoes, and bootees.[97] The prisoners in the camp were divided into eight groups, and were under a non-commissioned officer of the 54th.[98] Murray adds that seventy-five prisoners were in each letter A, B, C, etc. Furthermore, he says that the prisoners were numbered such as 1, 2, 3, 4, etc.[99] Prisoners were identified easily by being numbered. The numbering system is also in force in our modern era.

In addition to the identifications of the prisoners, Captain Emilio described the prison camp where the enemy combatants were incarcerated. The account of Captain Emelio was similar to that of John

Ogden Murray, a prisoner of war at that prison camp. In 1905, Murray wrote that the prisoners of war were divided into eight detachments at the prison camp at Wagner Camp in Morris Island.[100] As a prisoner himself, he was well accustomed to the environment and regulation of the camp. His description of the prison camp is from his own observations. Similar to Murray, Captain Emelio was one of the black troops stationed at Morris Island, South Carolina. The accounts of these two eye witnesses reveals pertinent facts on the incarcerations of prisoners as well as the regulations enforced for prison discipline at that time. Furthermore, their accounts provide salient information on the conditions of prisoners at the prison camp at Morris Island, South Carolina.

Prison Camp Under Colonel Hallowell at Morris Island

Captain Emilio, of the 54th regiment of the Massachusetts Infantry, recorded pertinent information regarding the camp where prisoners of war were detained. In addition, he also described the types of prisoners arrested by his company during the war. A similar description of the prison at Morris Island was also described by Murray. The information related by Captain Emilio and Murray are authoritative because these two individual people were present at the prison site. Captain Emilio was there as a prison guard, and Murray as a prisoner. In regard to their records, both agree on many aspects. The camp's descriptions of Captain Emilio and Murray were authentic. The accounts of these two writers were not collected from documents or the narratives of soldiers, but from their own observations. According to Captain Emilio, the yard where the camp was built was 228 by 304 feet, and formed the fortified of pine post, ten feet above ground, supporting a platform from which sentinels could watch the prisoners. The "dead line" marked by a rope stretched on posts was twenty feet. Possibly, the camp was strongly defended to avoid a prisoner's escape as well as the infiltration from the Confederate soldiers hoping to assist with the escape of their comrades. For the wellbeing of the prisoners, tents were also furnished for them. Each tent accommodated four men. The tens were pitched and arranged in rows forming eight streets. The ground was clean, dry, and quartz sand.[101] The camp seems to be well managed because there were regulations which the prison guards as well as the prisoners had to observe.

Murray elucidates that "the prison stockade was built of long pine poles driven in the sound and cleared together by pine boards. About the top of the high fence was a poropet built that the black guards might overlook our camp. This pen enclosed about two acres of land. On the inside of the Stockade fence, about ten feet from it, was stretched in a rope, the rope being supported on pickets driven into the sand. This was designated the dead line for a prisoner to approach this line, on any pretext, was sure death. The sentinels were ordered to shoot him without hesitation on challenge. The space between the dead line and fence curtailed the space on our Stockade prison very much. At the head of the middle street was placed a Mitailleuse Regua gun, loaded and ready to open upon our camp at a moment's notice. All this precautions were taken for fear we would overpower the black guards and capture this Island."[102] Through the illustration of Murray, it is sound to note that prison camps were fortified in a manner similar to modern prisons. Prison escapes were taken into consideration when such facilities were built.

Regulations in the Prison Camp

In the camp, prisoners were regulated with strict discipline. They had some liberty to move freely for a certain period of time during the day. Moreover, they were entrusted with the policing of the camp. It is possible that loyal prisoners were given police duties, but those who exhibited risky behavior were less likely to be permitted police duties. To better understand the regulations, a guard read them to each company of prisoners because they had to observe the rules.[103] Reading the regulations of the camp showed that the institution was well organized for the welfare of the prisoners as well as for the guards. As a rule, prisoners were required to stay in the camp. The warden called the roll three times a day. Every prisoner was accounted for to the officer on duty for the day.[104] After dark, the prisoners were not allowed to enter the street except to go to the barrel sinks. During the day, they were permitted to circulate freely in the camp; but not in groups of more than ten prisoners.[105] It appears that Union soldiers took precautions fearing attacks from the prisoners while in a group; the officers feared being overpowered allowing the prisoners to escape. The guards on duty warned the prisoners to avoid agglomerating in a group of ten. When they were discovered in a group of ten, they were asked to disperse or be shot.[106] Murray who was a prisoner of war at Morris Island relates that the threat to fire upon prisoners who were warned to disperse was taken seriously by the black guards. On one occasion, says Murray, Colonel van Manning, Fulkerson and him were warned to disperse when two more Confederate prisoners of war joined them. The black sentinels ordered them twice to disperse, but the prisoners did not comply. When the sentinel increased the tone of his voice, Colonel Van Manning and his companion prisoners of war decided to disperse avoiding being shot by the sentinel.[107] Due to the ten person rule, it was difficult for the prisoners to form a crowd. Some prisoners behaved well fearing being punished by the guards. In the prison, guards also feared for their own lives because of potential attacks from Confederate prisoners. Due to this, African American soldiers were more likely to enforce rules and regulations without sentiment. Confederate soldiers who attempted to violate rules were possibly sanctioned accordingly. With respect to the regulations of the prison, Murray and Captain Emilio recorded valuable information on the history of military prisons during the Civil War. As a reminder, Captain Emilio was one of the African American guards at the camp and Murray was a Confederate prisoner at Morris Island. Both wrote about the housing of Confederate prisoners at Morris Island Camp. In addition to these two writers, information about the imprisonment of Confederate prisoners at Point Lookout prison was noted in the *Supplement to the Official Records of the Union and Confederate Armies*. The account of Murray in regard to the regulation of the prison was as follows:

1. Prisoners were not allowed to approach the dead line rope on any pretext. Failure to do so was death. The sentinels were ordered to shoot a prisoner who passed the line without hesitation or challenge.
2. Prisoners were not allowed to be in a crowd of ten or more together. The sentinel was to order them to disperse. If the order

was not immediately obeyed by the prisoners, the sentinel was instructed to fire into the crowd.

3. No light or fires were allowed in the camp at any time after taps were sounded. If a match was struck in the tents, the black sentinel was ordered to shoot into the tent where he saw the light.
4. The prisoners had to be divided into eight detachments, seventy-five in each, lettered A, B, C, etc. Each prisoner was numbered 1, 2, 3, 4, etc.
5. Each detachment was to be under a warden, who was detailed from the guard on duty.
6. The rules ordered three roll calls every day. The first at one hour after sunrise, the second at 12:00 P.M, and the third at one half hour before sunset. At these times the prisoners were counted by the wardens, and the reports were taken by the officer on duty at the Company Street.
7. Each warden was ordered that his quarter of his detachment were properly policed and detailed if necessary.
8. Sick call was scheduled at 9 o'clock in the morning each day.
9. There were two barrel sinks for each detachment which were placed on the flanks of the camp during the day, and night in the Company Streets.
10. The barrels were ordered to be emptied after each call.
11. No talking allowed after evening roll call, and no prisoner was allowed to leave the tent after the time except to obey the calls of nature.
12. During the day, the prisoners were allowed to the limits of the camp as marked by the rope running between the stockade and line of tents.
13. No person, except the guards and officers, were allowed to communicate with the prisoners without permission from superiors at the headquarters.[108]

Duties of the Guards in the Prison Camp

The guards were charged with the management of the camp. They were entrusted with purchasing writing materials, pipes, tobacco, and necessary clothing. They were also ordered to inspect prisoner's letters before dispatching it to the receiving parties.[109] In addition, the guards were ordered to cook for the prisoners. The hours for the meals were scheduled according to the rules. Breakfast was served at 7:00 in the morning, dinner at 12:00 PM, and supper at 5:00 PM and the prisoners were served under the direction of the provost marshal. According to Murray, the ratio consisted of four hardtack army crackers, often rotten and green with mold.[110] It is possible that the guards also ate the same food as the prisoners. In addition, other soldiers who resided in the camp were most likely served the same food as the prisoners.

As there were many types of prisoners, the guards were instructed to monitor with vigilance the prisoners with a strong conviction for the Confederate cause and for those who would escape if the opportunity arrived.[111] In the prison, the intentions of overpowering the black guards were always present. To illustrate, at Point Lookout Prison, the prisoners planned a revolution secretly hoping to take tent polls as arms, break through the stockade fence and kill every black soldier on the point. The revolution was planned because a black sentinel shot a crowd of prisoners who were around a pump.[112] As in the current correctional system, during the Civil War, the guards took care of the safety of the prisoners. For their own protection, they were ordered to carry their guns loaded and capped. If more than ten prisoners were seen together except at meal time they would have been fired upon by the sentinels.[113] In addition to guarding prisoners, soldiers were also entrusted with the guarding of government and private properties.

Jail Services after the War

In some states, after the war, African American soldiers were entrusted with jail duties. In the city of Victoria in the state of Texas, the control of the city jail was under African American soldiers. According to Charles William Ramsdell, under the leadership of Captain Spaulding, African American soldiers who controlled the jail at Victoria abused their power as they wished.[114] He also stipulated that these soldiers prevented the keeping of people of their own race in that jail. Ramsdell notes that civil authorities were denied the right of keeping African Americans or Northern law breakers. African American soldiers were also accused by the county judge of liberating two African Americans incarcerated in the jail. Two federal soldiers convicted of robbery were also released by them.[115] Moreover, the soldiers were also accused of arbitrarily imprisoning citizens. After the war, the municipal town governments in former Confederate states were under the jurisdiction of military officers. Law enforcement duties were also performed by Union soldiers.

Guarding Government and Private Properties

From the start of the Civil War to the end, both armies aggressively protected government and private properties such as the railroad, arm depots, hospitals, bridges, ports, harbors, and water highways. Like other soldiers, African Americans performed guard duties protecting the listed properties. Similarly, African American soldiers were entrusted with guarding construction trains, government stores and horses, wagon trains, government wood choppers, the quartermaster's department, post commissary, telegraph lines, and convalescent camps. In addition, war ships were also protected by the soldiers of each concerned party. During the war, military equipment was moved from time to time to planned destinations. Therefore securing lines of communication was critical for the execution of the war. The party that controlled the water highway and the railroad was in a better position to inflict pain on the enemy. Knowing the importance of lines of communications, Union generals, without delay, occupied the harbor of Hilton Head. In a similar way, the city of Nashville and Chattanooga were also occupied. In Nashville, the railroad system was quite developed. It was easy to move the equipment from one state to another. The connection of the Chattanooga railroad to other states was noted by John Towsend Trowbridge. According to him, the East Tennessee and Virginia Railroad connected with the Nashville and Chattanooga, with the Western and Atlantic, making the place [Knoxville] an important centre of Railroad communications.[116] This connection made Nashville and Chattanooga important centers of military communications during the Civil War.[117] For the reasons noted above, Union commanders entrusted African American soldiers with the security of the railroads. As loyal military associates for the cause of the Union, African American soldiers were well-fitted to stand the harassment of the Confederate guerilla tactics. From the letter written by L. Thomas Pierce, Adjutant General to Hon. Edwin M. Stanton, the contents of the letter indicated that the lines of Nashville and Northwestern Railroads were guarded by the 12th and 13th Regiment. In like manner, the line of railroads from Nashville to Decatur, Alabama were guarded by black soldiers raised by General Dodge.[118]

Protecting property was one of the duties the War Department ordered African Americans to execute when they were permitted to enlist in the army. On August 25, 1862 when the Department of War authorized General Saxton who was in command of Port Royal to organize battalions of people of the African descent for the services of the Union, the department also entrusted black soldiers with guarding the plantations and settlements occupied by the United States. In addition, the protection of the inhabitants from captivity was part of the duties of the colored troops ordered by the Department of War.[119] The protection of Union properties such as arms warehouses, railroads, cotton plantations and cotton belonging to private people were beneficial to the execution of the war. Historians believe that the Union was successful in the war's execution due to their mastery and ownership of the lines of communication. They were able to attack the Confederates from various strategic points.

In 1862, the War Department ordered the enlistment of African Americans in the service of the United States but the number was not to be more than fifty thousand men. From this order, it is plausible to suggest that from the beginning of the Civil War until its end, Union soldiers were assigned with military police duties in guarding government properties such as military trains, depots, railroad, and employees. The protections of railroads was very critical for the success of the war. Civil War materials, personnel, and military accommodations were transported by trains. In addition, railroad patrol was also possibly conducted by train. Without access to railroads, the Union as well as the Confederates would be incapable of moving equipment in areas where water highways were nonexistent. Even in the regions such as Nashville, Tennessee, where River Cumberland was essential for the transportation of goods, the use of railroads by Union soldiers was critical. Therefore, for better movement of goods through the railroads, a better military guard was needed. To illustrate, in 1863, the 55th United States Colored Infantry stationed at Corinth, Mississippi was charged with the guarding of the railroad bridge on the United States military railroad which traveled from Memphis, Tennessee, to Corinth, Mississippi. Company A of this regiment, which was entrusted with the guarding of the railroad bridges, was in a camp at Pocahontas, Tennessee.[120] Similarly, Company G of the same regiment, that was stationed at Port Hudson, Louisiana, was sent to Bill Hill, Tennessee, to guard bridges on the Memphis Charleston Railroad.[121] Company H of the 55th United States Colored Infantry was charged with guarding the wagon train.[122] In Mississippi, Dunbar Rawland notes that white and black soldiers guarded the posts and communication lines, as well as steamers.[123] The same information was recorded by Whitelaw Reid.[124]

While the 55th United States Colored Infantry was in charge of guarding the bridges, Company D of the 56th United States Colored Infantry was stationed at Helena, Arkansas and guarded government wood choppers by the order of Brigadier General N. B. Buford, who commanded the Eastern District of Arkansas. A similar infantry force assigned with guarding the government wood yard was the 56th United States Colored Company D; this force was stationed at Island No.63, Mississippi while they were guarding the wood yard.[125]

Company B of the 56th United States Infantry was assigned with guarding government stores at the post at Helena, Arkansas. The men of this company were credited for being efficient and faithful in their performance of their daily duties. Company H and G were on special assignment guarding the quartermaster's stores.[126] The 81st United States Colored Infantry (formerly the 4th Regiment, United States Volunteers and 9th Regiment Infantry, Corps d'Afrique) selected Company C to guard the General Hospital at New Orleans.[127] Another black infantry entrusted to guard the patients was the 89th United States Colored Infantry which was stationed at Port Hudson. Soldiers of this regiment were on guard duty at the Convalescent Camp at Port Hudson. In addition to guarding properties, black soldiers were also ordered to guard people. Many southerners disliked being guarded by black soldiers; they believed this was disgraceful.[128]

During the execution of the Civil War, African Americans were entrusted with law enforcement duties in the rebel states. They were employed as guard and military police for the prevention of peace and the maintenance of order. In addition, they were empowered with correctional duties in the prison camps as well as in the city jail under the jurisdiction of the Union. Even though they acted as such, African slaves and freemen were disliked by Southerners, expecially their masters. After the war, they were mustered out of the United States army and could not serve. Law enforcement duties entrusted to African slaves and freemen differed from town to town or region to region. In areas where their presence was opposed, they served only as guards. This was the case in Nashville, Tennessee. On the contrary, in Memphis, they were empowered with military police duties. Like in Memphis, in Louisiana and South Carolina, they were also entrusted with military police duties during the execution of the Civil war as well as the occupations of those states by Union soldiers. In Mississippi and Florida, they also acted the same.

Notes

1   Luis F Emilo, *History of the Fifty-Fourth Regiment of Massachusetts Volunteer Infantry, 1863-1865*. Boston Book Company, 1894.

2   Robert Alonzo Brock, See Southern Historical Society papers, vol. 1-2. p. 232. From the diary of Captain Robert Park, of Twelfth Alabama regiment, Brock collected the data which revealed that black soldiers were respectful to their former masters. Even while they were prisoners, black soldiers called them masters.

3   Ibid.

4   Letter of W. Hoffman, Colonel Third Infantry and Commissary of Prisoners to Hon. E.M. Stanton, Secretary of War, Washington, D.C. Written at Point Lookout, May 20, 1864. See Compilation of the Official Record

of the Union and Confederate Armies. U.S. Government Printing Office, 1899, pp.153-154.

5   See "Point Lookout Prison" in Watson's magazine, Vol.13. Jeffersonian Publishing Company, 1911, p.340.

6   Ibid.

7   John Ogden Murray, *The Immortal Six Hundred: A Story of Cruelty to Confederate Prisoners of War*. Eddy Press, 1905, p.84.

8   Ibid, p.92.

9   Ibid, p.94.

10 Janet B. Hewett, *Suppliment to the Official Records of the Union and Confederate Armies*. Part II of Events vol.78. U.S. Colored Troops Serial No. 90. Broadford Publishing Company, Wilmington, NC, 1998.

11 Jefferson Davis, *A Short History of the Confederate States of America*, New York Belford Company, Publishers, 1890, p.76.

12 The seceding states formed a provisional Constitution for the new Confederate under the style of the Confederate States of America. The Constitution was adopted and continued for a year. In addition, the permanent Constitution was adopted. The Constitution of the Confederate of States of America was modeled on the Constitution of the United States, with only such changes. See Jefferson Davis, *A Short History of the Confederate States of America*. New York Belford Company Publishers, 1890, pp.60, 65.

13 Ibid, p,61.

14 See Francis J. Lieber, *The Miscelaneous Writings of Francis Lieber*. J.B. Lippincott & Company, 1881.

15 See Ibid., p.257.

16 Charles Carleton Coffin, *Stories of Our Soldiers: War Reminiscences*, vol.2 Pub. By the Journal Newspaper Company, 1893, p.17 General Butler held the slaves of Colonel Malloy because the state of Virginia passed the ordinance of the secession. Therefore, the state was no longer part of the United States. It belonged to a foreign nation which was the Confederate country to be.

17 Thomas Wentworth Higginson, *Army Life in a Black Regiment*. Boston: Fields, Osgood & CO, 1870, p.2.

18 Coffin, 1893, p.17.

19 Susie King Taylor, *Reminiscence of my Life in Camp with the 33rd United States Colored Troops*. The author, 1902, p.51.

20 Ibid.

21 See Letter written at the Headquarter. Northern District, Department of the South. Edisto, May 6, 1862 by H. W. Benham to Jules De La Croix, Esq. U.S. Agent in charge of Contrabands. The War of the Rebellion: V-1-5 [Serial No. 122 – 126] Correspondence, orders, reports and return of the Union authorities, United States, War Dept. Henry Martin Lazelle, Leslie J. Perry. U.S. Government printing, 1899, p.30.

22 Ibid, p.31.

23 See Proclamation of Major General Hunter made in Hilton Head, S.C., May 9, 1862.

24 See Letter of Edward L. Pierce, Special Agent Treasury Department to Hon. S. P. Chase written in Port Royal , S.C. May 12, 1862. See the War of the rebellion: V.1-5 [Serial No 122 -126, Correspondence, orders, reports and return of the Union authorities, 1899, p.30.

25 See Laura Joseph Webster, The Operation of the Freedmen's Bureau in South Carolina, vol. 1, issue 2. Department of History of Smith College, 1916, p.69.

26 The First Kansas Colored Regiment was established earlier than other listed black regiments. But this regiment was mustered in the United States after that of the regiment formed by Colonel Higginson.

27 Higginson, 1870, pp.1-2, Higginson always advocated for the arming of black people, and felt the wish to be associated with such soldiers.

28 Luis Fenollosa Emilio notes that John A. Andrew, the war governor of Massachusetts, advocated very early for the enlistment of black men to aid in suppressing the rebellion. Governor Andrew was an abolitionist who believed in the end of slavery. For his communication with General Butler, See History of the Fifty-Fourth regiment of Massachusetts Volunteer Infantry, 1863 – 1865, Boston Book Company, 1894, p.239.

29 James Parton, *General Butler in New Orleans: History of the Administration of Gulf in the year 1862*, 1864, pp.64-65.

30 Horace Greeley, *The American Conflict: A History of the Great Rebellion in the United States of America, 1850 – 65,* its causes, incidents, and Results intended to exhibit especially, it Moral , Case, 1866. General Lorenzo also visited Memphis, Helena, and other parts were blacks migrated. p.526.

31 John Stevens Cabot Abbott, *The History of the Civil War in America*, L. Bill, 1866, p.290.

32 See The Memphis Riot, 1866, Congressional Editions, vol.7985, 1922, p.92.

33 See Emilio, 1894, pp.5-6.

34 Taylor, 1902, p.16.

35 Frederick Douglass, *Life and times of Frederick Douglass*. Park Publishing, 1882, p.418.

36 See Congressional Edition, vol.7985, The Mephis Riot May 1-3, 1866, U.S. Government Printing Office, 1922, pp.92-93.

37 See Janet B. Hewett, *Supplement to the Official Records of the Union and Confederate Armies. Part II. Record of Events*, vol.27. U.S. Colored Troops. Broodfoot Publishing Company, NC, 1998, pp.101, 117,157, 193, 425,436, 512, 515, 519, 602.

38 Carlos Emmor Godfrey, *The Commanding-in-Chief's Guard*, Revolutionary War. Stevenson-Smith Company, 1904, P.19.

39 Ibid. The small squads of cavalrymen were occasionally detailed for a brief period to escort Washington upon long journeys, or to serve as an auxiliary guard of his person in times of action, p.14.

40 The provost position was established under the resolution of Congress of May 27, 1778. See John Blair Linn and William Henry Egle, Pennsylvania Archives, Pennsylvania in the War of Revolution, Battalions and Line, 1775 – 1783, vol.2, See Von Heer's Light Dragoons. p.171.

41 Ibid.

42 Frank Moore, *The Rebellion Record: A Dairy of American Events, with Documents, Narratives, Illustrative Incidents, Poetry, &C.*, G.P. Putnam, 1864, p.523.

43 Ibid.

44 Emilio, 1894, p.280.

45 See War department order, Washington City, D.C. August 25, 1862, Higginson, 1870, p.273.

46 Ibid, p.279.

47 Ibid.

48 Ibid, pp.57 -58.

49 Ibid.

50 Ibid, p.109.

51 Ibid, 62.

52 David Dixon Porter, *The Naval History of the Civil War*. Courier Dover Publications, 1886, p.86.

53 Ibid.

54 Ellis Paxson Oberholtzer, *A History of the United States since the Civil War*, vol.1. Macmillan, 1917, p.94.

55 Higginson, 1870, p.57.

56 Hewett, *Supplement to the Official Records of the Union and Confederate Armies, Part II of Events* vol. 78. U.S. Colored Troops, Serial No. 90. Bradford Publishing Company, Washington, NC, 1998, p.558.

57 Ibid, p.136.

58 Congressional Edition, vol. 7985, The Memphis, Tennessee, Riots, 1866. U.S. Government Printing Office, 1922, p.92.

59 See House Documents, Vol.223 – 224, Memphis Riots and Massacres July 25, 1866. U.S. Government Printing Office, 1866, p.31.

60 Ibid.

61 See Report of the Committees of House of Representative of the Memphis riots in 1866, p.6.

62 Ibid.

63 John MCleod Keating and O.F. Vedder, *History of the City of Memphis and Shelby County Tennessee: With Illustrations and Biographical Sketches of Some of Its Prominent Citizens*, vol.1. D. Mason & Company, 1888, p.568 Same information was also recorded by A.R. James, Standard History of Memphis, Tennessee: From a Study of the Originial Sources. H.W. Crew, 1912, p.140.

64 Walter T. Durham, Reluctant Partners. Nashville and the Union July 1, 1863 to June 30, 1865. The Tennessee Historical Society. Nashville, 1987.

65 Henry Martyn Lazelle and Leslie J. Perry, The War of the Rebellion: A Compilation of the Official Records of the Union and Confederate Armies. United States War Department, 1889, p.479. Letter from U.S. Grant to Major Gen. J. B. Mcpherson, Cpmmanding Seventeenth Army Corps of July 5, 1863. See also Congressional Serial Set. U.S. Government Printing Office, 1891, p.479.

66 Hewett, 1998,p. 159.

67 David Dixon Porter, The Naval History of the Civil War. Sherman Pub. Company, 1886, p.330.

68 Evert Augustus Duyckink, National History of the War for the Union, Civil, Military and Naval: Founded on Official and Other Authentic Documents, vol.1, Johnson, Fry, 1861, p.118.

69 Ibid, p.403.

70 See The Memphis Riot, May 1-3, 1866. Congressiona Edition, vol.7985. U.S. Government Printing Office, 1922, pp.92-92.

71 Ibid, p.130.

72 Ibid, p.136.

73 Emilio, 1894, p.312.

74 Hewett, 1998, vol.27, p.433.

75 See The United States Congressional Serial Set, Issue 3436, 1896, p.223, The Memphis Riots of 1866.

76 See Sussie Taylor King, *Reminiscences of my Life in Camp with the 33rd United States Colored Troops,* The author, 1902.

77 Susie Taylor King, *Reminiscences of my Life in Camp with the 33rd United States Colored Troops*, The author, 1902, p.42.

78 Ibid.

79 Charles Carleton, *Four Years of Fighting*, Ticknor and Fields, 1866, p.49.

80 Ibid.

81 John Stevens Cabot Abbott, *The History of the Civil War in America*. L. Bill, 1866, p.291.

82 Emilio, 1894, p.312.

83 Hewett, 1998, vol.78, p.503.

84 Ibid, p.358.

85 Emilio, 1894, p.222.

86 Hewett, 1998, p.239, vol.78.

87 Murray, 1905, p.84.

88 Emilio, 1894, p.218.

89 Murray, 1905, p.88.

90 Ibid, p,90.

91 Thomas Edward Watson, Watson's Magazine, vol.5. Jefferson Publishing Company, 1911, p.340.

92 Hewett, 1988, pp.544-558, vol.78.

93 Ibid, 1988, p.107, vol.27.

94 Ibid, p.157, vol.27.

95 Ibid, p.366, vol.78.

96 Emilio, 1894, p.224.

97 Ibid, p.222.

98 Ibid.

99 Murray, 1905, p.97.

100 Murray, 1905, p.94.

101 Emilio, 1894, pp.222-224.

102 Murray, 1905, pp.94-95.

103 Emilio, 1894, p.224.

104 Ibid.

105 Ibid.

106 Ibid.

107 Murray, 1905, p.96.

108 Ibid, p.97.

109 Emilio, 1894, p.224.

110 Murray, 1905, p.99.

111 Emilio, 1894, p.224.

112 Watson, 1911, p.340.

113 Ibid, p.98.

114 Charles William Ramsdell, *The Reconstruction in Texas.* New York, Columbia University, 1910, pp.130-131.

115 Ibid.

116 John Townsend Trowbridge, *A Tour of its Battle Field and Ruined Cities, a Journey through the Desolated States, and Talks with the People,* 1867, p.248.

117 Ibid.

118 See Letter of L. Thomas Pierce, Adjutant General to Hon. Edwin M. Stanton, Secretary of War. The account was collected from the Compilation of the Official Records of the Union and Confederate Armies. U.S. Government Printing Office, 1902, p.4433.

119 Higginson, 1870, p.273.

120 Hewett, 1998, vol.78, p.256.

121 Ibid, p.264.

122 Ibid, p.266.

123 Danbar Rawland, *War and Reconstruction in Mississippi.* See J.S. MCNeily, Publications of the Mississippi Historical Sciety, 1918, 175.

124 Whitelaw Reid, *After the War, Moore:* Westoch & Baldwin, 1866, p.279.

125 Hewett, 1998, p.315.

126 Ibid, pp.311, 312.

127 Ibid, p.653.

128 Ried, 1866, p.297.

129 See National Park Service. Fort Davis National History Site. African Americans in the Frontier Army.

130 Lieutenant Grote Hutchinson, Adjutant 9th U.S. Cavalry, The Ninth Regiment of Cavalry.

131 Ibid.

132 Ibid.

133 See the National Park Service, Fort Davis National Historic Site. From the National Park, we find that the primary mission of the regiment at Fort Davis was the protection of travelers and the mail on the San Antonio – El Paso Road. They also scouted and patrolled the vast trans – Pecos region of western Texas.

134 Report of the Committees of the House of Representatives for the First Session of the Forty – Third Congress. The Ninth Cavalry is in Texas. Government Printing Office, 1874, p.8.

135 Frank Lincoln Mather, *Who's Who of the Colored Race.* Publisher not identified, 1915, p.15.

CHAPTER VI

Law and Order in the Blacks' Civil War Settlements and Villages

The War of Secession transformed the lives of African Americans in different ways that included brutal separations with their masters, conflicts with their former owners, dependency on the federal government, and their citizenship status. Similar to other soldiers, freedmen received privileges of serving in the American army. They received the same training as their white counterparts. By being mustered in the service of the United States, they were capable of performing all military services required of soldiers during war time. As military men, United States government officials were obligated to secure their family members and freed African Americans. During the war, African Americans were protected in the army camps or settlements formed for them by high ranking United States soldiers. Before this period, they were under the governership of the plantation owners. On the contrary, during the war and thereafter, they were included in the American body politic.

The inclusion of African Americans in the American body politic did not happen in a vacuum or in isolation. Colonel Thomas Wentworth Higginson believed that "till the blacks were armed, there was no guarantee of their freedom. It was their demeanor under arms that shamed the nation into recognizing them as men."[1] In this status, they were allowed to hold minor offices in the villages or settlements organized for them by United States high-ranking officials. This was the case of Mitchelville in South Carolina.

It is known that before the war, African slaves in the United States were property of men. They were not considered citizens. On the contrary, during the war, they were protected by the Union. As dependents of the Union, they were given some opportunities to regulate their personal affairs through legal mechanisms in settlements built for them. Therefore, a government of the blacks by the blacks was formed in the land chartered for them by General Ormsby Mitchel of Ohio in South Carolina. To honor General Mitchel, the village was named Mitchelville.[2] At the time when General Mitchel was in contact with African Americans, there was a large population of contraband in Hilton Head and in the surrounding villages. It is not known whether Freedmen around Hilton Head went to reside in Mitchelville. According to Whitelaw Reid, Mitchelville was formed by freedmen who regulated and organized a local government for the village.[3] Isaiah Price notes that the contraband's settlement of Mitchelville was built by "the blacks of rough boards and slabs received at [a] sawmill which was worked by men detailed to provide lumber for general purposes."[4] Surely, as freedmen were not self-sufficient, they were incapable of establishing a town. Therefore, United States government officials sponsored the building of Mitchelville.

The Village of Mitchelville

The little village of Mitchelville was designed to serve as recompense to African Americans for their loyalty to the Union. It is difficult to ascertain whether or not it was an experimental action. The historic government of Mitchelville is of importance to the public. It is pertinent to relate to readers how Mitchelville was governed by African Americans. According to Whitelaw Reid, the village was organized and regulated by a mayor, common council, marshall, recorder, and treasurer who were all African Americans.[5] The organization and regulation of the village was totally under the control of African Americans. This was the first local black government under the flag of the United States. Before the Civil War, there were villages and settlements governed by blacks in the United States, but they were not under the rule of the American government. On the contrary, Mitchelville was a recognized municipal village of blacks in the United States with full support from Union soldiers. Moreover, it was also in this village that African Americans were authorized to elect one of their own as mayor and treasurer. Reid does not discuss the conditions set for the elections of the mayor and treasurer in Mitchelville. Furthermore, there is no data revealing that influential black people in the village elected the mayor and the recorder. Possibly, the mayor was elected by the black aldermen. As the mayor and the treasurer were elected by blacks, it seems that other officers were appointed by Union soldiers. It's essential to note that United States soldiers ruled the village indirectly through black village officials. Even though his name is not recorded, the mayor of Mitchelville was the first person of African descent to hold that position in the United States. At the time of the writing of this book, there is no data indicating that an African American was elected mayor in an American city or village prior to the Civil War. Even though Mitcheville had a mayor, there is no record that the city was chartered. Mitchelville was named for the rememberance of General Ormsby M. Mitchel, a friend of African Americans and the first architect of that village. He died before the beginning of Mitchelville's construction.[6]

Mitchelville has been called by various names such as village, contraband settlement, and town. In this locality, United States military forces were very involved with its security, political affairs and economy. Reed recorded pertinent information of the enforcement of Mitchelville. Reed writes that military orders were enforced for the purpose of executing the village's affairs. The orders recorded by Reed for the governing of Mitchelville were as follows:

1. All lands now set apart for the colored population, near Hilton Head, are declared to constitute a village, to be known as the village of Mitchelville. Only freedmen and colored persons residing or sojourn within the teritorial limits of said village, shall be deemed and considered inhabitants thereof.

2. The village of Mitchelville shall be organized and governed as follows: said village shall be divided into districts, as nearly equal in population as practicable, for the election of councilmen, sanitary and police regulations and the general government of the people therein.

3. The government shall consist of a supervisor and treasurer, to be appointed by, and hold office during the pleasure of the military commander of the district, assisted by a councilman from each council district, to be elected by the people, who shall also, at the same time, choose a recorder and Marshal. The duties of the Marshal and Recorder shall be defined by the Council of Administration.

4. The Supervisor and Councilmen shall constitute the Council of Administration, with the recorder as Secretary.

5. The Council of Administration shall have power: "to pass such ordinances as it shall deem best, in relation to the following subjects: To establish schools for the education of children and other persons. To prevent and punish vagrant idles, and crime. To punish licentiousness, drunkenness, offenses against public decency and good order, and petty violation of the right of property and person. To require due observance of the Lord's Day. To collect fines and penalties. To punish offenses against village ordinances. To settle and determine disputes concerning claims for wages, personal property, and controversies between debtor and creditor. To levy and collect taxes and to defray the expenses of the village government, and for the support of schools. To layout regulate, and clean the streets. To establish wholesome sanitary regulations for the prevention of disease. Appoint officers, places and times for the holding of elections. To compensate municipal officers, and to regulate all other matters affecting the well-being of citizens and good order of society.

6. Hilton Head Island will be divided into school districts to conform, as nearly as practibly to the schools as established by the Freemen's Association. In each district there shall be elected one school commissioner, who will be charged with supplying the wants of the schools under the direction of the teacher thereof. "[7]

It appears that the Council of Administration had legislative and judiciary power. As legislative officers, they passed the ordinances of the town. The judiciary power they had was in adjudicating civil and criminal cases. As law enforcers, they were also regulators of the town because the control of taxes was under their jurisdiction. Additionally, they had executive power to appoint minor law enforcement officers.

As the town or village was populated by African Americans, it is plausible to note that the entire Council of Administration of Mitchelville was composed of African descendants.

School Attendance in Mitchelville

In Mitcheville, education was highly valued by African Americans. A compulsory school system was enforced in this village; in each school district students were ordered to attend school days during the sessions, except in cases of sickness. Similarly, with the permission of the parents, children of legal working age were excused from missing school sessions with written excuses from the teacher and approved by the school district. In this case, the parents or guardians were accountable for the return of students who missed school in the following sessions or face a penalty at the discretion of the Council of Administration.[8]

The ordinances, regulations, and the organization of Mitchelville educate us that all the components of the criminal justice system were in place. There was a court, correction, and a police system. In addition, regulatory agents were also active in the village for the collection of taxes and regulation of sanitation and schools. The Council of Administration had a broad power such as judiciary, executive, and legislative as we learned from the military order. In addition, they also had regulatory power such as tax collection. Possibly, the marshal enforced the ordinances of the village. In addition to Michelville, the little village of the Contraband deserves notice because the said village was under the control of freedmen.

The Little Contraband Village in Chattanooga

In Chattanooga, black people had their own settlement during the Civil War. This settlement was a little village of huts formed of slaves who ran away from their masters. African Americans who escaped from their masters during the Civil War were called contrabands. The term contraband was used the first time by General Butler while at the Potomac in Virginia. Charles Carleton Coffin tells us that the first contraband appeared into the line of the Union Army of the Potomac in 1861. According to him, Sam Allston, the slave of Allston, was the first contraband of the Civil War. His master, Allston, was a resident of Fairfax, South Carolina and a soldier in the South Carolina Regiment of the Confederate.

As for the population of African Americans in and around Chattanooga, John Towsend Trowbridge writes that "there were three thousand blacks."[9] He collected the African American census from the account of Captain Lucas, of the Freedmen's Bureau.[10] Possibly due to the population of the free blacks, a village was also formed for their interests and protection. In regard to the Chattanooga Village, Trowbridge tells us that it was situated on the north side of the river. The village was ruled by a president and council chosen by African Americans.[11] The selected officials were more likely honorable people with good moral characters. In this village, a court was ruled by the officials chosen by blacks. The president and the council adjudicated minor violations. The black court in Chattanooga was under the control of the Freedmen's Bureau. The African American's court decisions were credited by Captain Lucas. In his view, African American adjudicators made wise and just decision in their court rulings.[12] The assessment of Captain Lucas on the African American's court rulings was based on his own experience. He was an eye witness and had first-hand knowledge on the administration of the African Americans' village. Furthermore, Captain Lucas was also a participant in some cases. He informed Trowbridge that "he had to interfere, sometimes, however, to mitigate the severity of the sentence." He also went on to inform him that "these men showed no prejudice in favor of their own color, but meted out a rugged and austere justice to all."[13] From the account of Trowbridge, we can speculate that black judges and other officers adjudicating legal cases were impartial. It appears judges were prone to keeping the harmony within the village. Injustice and partiality within their legal system would destroy the fabric of the village.

In regard to the black villages, there were possibly many villages in southern states that were governed by African Americans during the Civil War. James Parton, who wrote about General Butler in 1864, also noted that there was a large population of people of African American descent in the village of Hampton, Virginia. These African Americans were hired in various assignments such as in the military as well as civil.[14] Unlike Virginia, in South Carolina there were villages under the control of African Americans. G. Campbell, an African American, was the self-proclaimed ruler of a settlement in South Carolina.

The Government of Tunis G. Campbell

In South Carolina, where the population of escaped slaves was high, the United States government used military officials as well as volunteers from the North to organize many social programs to assist the newly freed African Americans. General Saxton, the architect of those programs did not exclude blacks from being employed in the Freedmen Bureau. We find that Tunis G. Campbell, an African American from Canada, was appointed agent of the Bureau by General Saxton.[15] Contrary to the account of Thompson, in the Senate Document, Campbell was listed as an African American from New York City. Before the Civil War, it was common for African Americans to escape to Canada to avoid slavery. This African American according to W.E.B. Du Bois was born in Massachusetts.[16] Dr. Du Bois mentioned the state where he was born but did not specify the city.

Campbell was not only an agent of the Freedmen Bureau, but an influential African American who ruled and administered some coastal islands with the assistance of some black leaders. Clara Mildred Thompson notes that "Campbell set up an autocratic government with an absurdly elaborate Constitution, senate, house of representatives, courts of various kinds, with himself as chief autocrat."[17] As Campbell established the judiciary system, he appointed judges for that purpose. Judges were possibly selected from influential and affluent blacks in the islands. Campbell, being an autocrat leader, appointed his judges at will. His friends were possibly included in the magistracy of his courts. The formation of Savannah's coastal government was also mentioned by W.E.B. Du Bois in 1935.[18] As an educated African American, Campbell's leadership was well investigated before Dr. Du Bois would refer to it as a government. It seems that Dr. Du Bois found concrete evidence of an existing government in the territory held by Campbell.

Similar accounts were also given in the Senate document. In the consulted documents, Campbell ruled St. Catherine's Island, Ossabow, and Sopelo.[19] The Senate document described him as being "a person of great plausibility and remarkable cunning." On these islands, the exploitation of woods was under his control. The woods he cut were sold to passing steamers. Money generated from selling wood was for his profits as well as his fellow leaders who believed in his government. He was also accused by the Senate of not paying freedmen who assisted him with cutting woods.[20] As ruler of the islands, the protection of the islands' government was given more weight.

Campbell employed his influence by denying access to any white landowners who planned to visit the islands, except for the agents of the Freemen Bureau. Anticipating the entrance of white people in the islands, he ordered his armed guard to prevent such entry. He hired twenty-five black men armed with U.S. muskets as a measure of prevention to prevent whites from entering the settlements.[21] On St. Catherine's Island, Campbell controlled 515 acres of land scattered over the island. It also appears that the city of Darien was under the jurisdiction of Campbell. W.E.B. Du Bois agreed that when Tunis Campbell settled in Darien, he controlled all the blacks who lived in that city. He went on to say that he ruled them also.[22]

Black Watchmen on St. Simon's Island

During the war, on St. Simon's Island, African Americans were the majority. It looks like white people were absent in that territory. According to the report of E. I. Pierce, Government Agent, "when a district of Ladies' Island left exposed, African Americans carried arms when they bought, and acted as sentries." According to the statement of Agent Pierce, African Americans were the protectors of their own people on the island. As sentries, they performed guard and police duties for the welfare of the residents. Similarly, in North Edisto, in the colony of African Americans, the security of the district was assured by themselves. Pierce notes that "armed African Americans drove back the rebel cavalry." On St. Simon's Island, Susie Taylor King who visited the island with soldiers noted that "there were no soldiers in 1862 at the time of their arrival." Blacks acted as watchmen for the security of their families against the attacks of the Confederate rebels. During patrol duties, Charles O'Neal lost his life. O'Neil was the leader of the blacks and the uncle of Edward King, the husband of Susie Taylor King, a sergeant in Company E of the United States Colored Troops formerly the 1st South Carolina Volunteer Regiment of Thomas Wentworth Higginson. The island was formed of many settlements where African Americans resided. Possibly in all these settlements, African Americans carried arms to protect themselves against the Confederate rebels. According to the estimate of King, there were six hundred men, women, and children. The majority of the population were women and children.[23]

During the Civil War, African slaves were dependents of the federal government. Due to their support of the flag of the United States, there were privileged with some protections. Union soldiers organized settlements and towns for them. In these localities, they were allowed to form a government ruled by themselves. In such settlements or villages, law enforcement officers were people of the African race.

Notes

1 Thomas Wentworth Higginson, *The Writings of Thomas Wentworth Higginson: Army Life in a Black Regiment*. Reverside Press, 1900, p.359.

2 Whitelaw Reid, *After the War: A Southern Tour*, May 1, 1865, to May 1, 1866, p.89.

3 Ibid.

4 Isaiah Price, *History of the Ninety-Seventh Regiment, Pennsylvania Volunteer Infantry, During the War of the Rebellion, 1861 – 65*, 1875, p.130.

5 Whitetaker Reid, *After the War: A Southern Tour: May 1, 1865, to May 1, 1866*. Moore Wilstach & Baldwin, 1866, pp.89-90.

6 Ibid.

7 Ibid.

8 Ibid.

9 John Towsend Trowbridge, *A Tour of its Battlefields and ruined cities, a journey through the Desolated states, and talks with the people, 1867,* L. Stibbins, 1866, p.251.

10 Ibid.

11 Ibid, p.252.

12 Ibid.

13 Trowbridge, 1867, p.252.

14 James Parton, *General Butler in New Orleans: History of the Administration of Gulf in the Years 1862, 1864,* p.164.

15 Clara Mildred Thompson, *Reconstruction in Georgia.* Columbia University Press, 1915, p.59.

16 W.E.B. Du Bois, *Black Reconstruction in America, 1860 – 1880.* Simon and Schuster, 1935, p.499.

17 Ibid.

18 W.E.B. Du Bois and Daid Leveering Lewis, 1935, p.427.

19 See Senate documents for the islands ruled by Campbell. The Senate documents listed that Ossobow, St. Catherine, and Sopelo Island were under the control of Tunis G. Campbell. Senate Documents, Otherwise Pub. As Public Documents and Executive Documents: 14th Congress, 1st, Organization of the labor on the Sea Islands, 1867, p.52.

20 Ibid.

21 See *Columbia Studies in the Social Science,* Columbia University Press, 1915, p.57, Colored Troops in Darien.

22 W.E.B. Du Bois and David Levering Lewis, 1935, p.499.

23 Susie King Taylor, *Reminiscences of my Life in Camp with the 33rd United States Colored Troops:* late 1st S.C. Volunteers, the author, 1902, pp. 12-14.

CHAPTER VII

African American Spies, Scouts, and Informants in the War of Secession

The War of Secession was not only fought with weapons, human intelligence was also an instrument of war. From the beginning of the war, African Americans, like other people, furnished information to the Union regarding the movement, location, and some known war plans of the Confederate rebels. In addition, escaped African American slaves revealed to the Union officials the contributions made by people of their own color to the Confederate Army. From the arrival of the first contraband slaves, General Benjamin Franklin Butler learned that African Americans were used for the construction of fortifications in the areas controlled by the Confederate army.[1] In like manner, they informed General Butler that African Americans were used to set battery for the rebels.[2] From this information, General Butler was forced to implement a policy regarding escaped slaves that was not planned by the United States government. Hoping to prevent rebels from using the labor of African Americans, he welcomed runaway slaves and freed those who came to the Union lines. He also employed them for the benefit of the Union. The first contraband slaves were employed for the construction of fortifications. Even though General Butler welcomed runaway slaves, there were pro-slavery generals who sent African slaves away from the Union lines.

Escaped slaves and other African Americans were great assets to the Union. Government officials such as the Secretary of War, Mr. Stanton, knew the importance of African Americans' assistance.

When General Ormsby M. Mitchel requested the formation of African American regiments, the Secretary of War noted to him that "the assistance of slaves was an element of military strength which [...] he was fully justified in employing."[3] This statement indicates that government officials believed that African Americans were Union allies. Like government officials, abolitionist generals such as Thomas W. Higginson, John C Fremont, John W. Phelps, Francis G. Shaw, and Colonel James Montgomery, championed the employment of African Americans in the army during the Civil War. These generals also advocated for the protection of African Americans.

During the Civil War, spying and scouting were observed by Col. Lafayette Baker and Allen Pinkerton as well as Sarah Emma Evelyn Edmonds. These noted authors discussed the concept of spying and scouting during the Civil War. Col. Lafayette Charles Baker and Allan Pinkerton discovered that much intelligence gathering and trespassing into the enemy's territory was conducted regularly by spies and scouts. The mission of spies was to collect information on the movement of the rebels, fortifications, and military equipment as well as their origin. Similarly, sometimes Civil War spies gave an estimate number of the Confederate soldiers to the Union soldiers before conducting an attack. Possibly, spies and scouts documented the geographical conditions of the enemy's locations to facilitate the entrance of Union men. The assignments of spies as listed by Pinkerton included "entering the rebel lines and endeavoring to obtain accurate information of the nature of their defenses, the number of troops under their command at various points, etc . . ." It appears that spies entering rebel lines were frequently in search of accurate war data.

In the beginning of the Civil War, Col. Lafayette Charles Baker and Allan Pinkerton employed many people to collect, gather, and analyze documents from the enemy's territories. The analysis of collected documents was critical for the planning of attacks as well as spying. The same methods were also utilized by the Confederate generals. For better collection and gathering of intelligence, it is important to refer to the Bureau of the National Detective Police. This bureau was estsblished during the Civil War and Col. Lafayette

Baker was the chief of this Bureau.[4] Like the Bureau of the National Detective Police, the United States Secret Service, which was organized by General McClellan during the Civil War, was under the control and management of Allan Pinkerton.[5] He was in fact the chief of the government's secret service.[6] The secret service spied on the Confederate authorities, associations, armed officials, and the traitors of the government of the United States. At the beginning of the Civil War, the city of Richmond, Virginia was the center where Confederate officials, soldiers, and spies met with hope of assassinating President Lincoln instead of carrying on with the war. In addition, this city was possibly where the rebels were planning how to capture Washington, the capital city, in the hopes of avoiding the war against the United States.

With the design of protecting the national capital and the president, Col. Lafayette Charles Baker utilized scouting and detection to accomplish his mission. On the other hand, Allan Pinkerton employed spying and scouting. In regard to scouting, Col. Charles Lafayette Bakers says that "the principal qualifications of scouts are courage and daring. The agents must enter deep into the enemy's lines, generally during the action, or while the army is in motion, to ascertain the locality and movement of the hostile forces." He went on to say that "the detective must possess abilities, shrewdness, great self-reliance, courage, and integrity."[7] As noted by Colonel Baker, spies took on hazardous and risky missions while penetrating the enemy's territory. The enemies severely punished those caught spying on them. In fact, many Union spies were killed by the Confederate soldiers.

Sarah Emma Evelyn Edmonds says that during the Civil War, scouting was done by volunteers in a "detached service" from the ranks that served as guides, undertook reconnaissance patrols, or went on missions in enemy territory.[8] The duties listed by Edmonds were also done by African American spies such as John Scobell and Harriet Tubman. The information regarding the duties of John Scobell and Harriet Tubman will be discussed later in this chapter. On the other hand, Edmonds explains that "spies were most often civilians who lived behind enemy lines and reported via secret messengers or travelled through hostile territory on assignment and then returned to their own lines."[9] The penetration of spy agents in the enemy lines were conducted by the agents of the secret service under the administration of Allan Pinkerton as well as the generals in the fields. In addition to spying and scouting, passing information to the Union was frequently done by the Union loyalists as well as their African American allies. Runaway slaves were frequently employed as spies during the Civil War. African Americans, as loyal supporters of the Union, believed in their deliverance from slavery. Therefore, it was plausible for them to make significant contributions towards that purpose.

United States Navy officials also benefited from African American informants and spies who were well acquainted with the rivers and swamps in the regions where they conducted their war missions. African Americans were not excluded from performing scouting and spying duties during the Civil War. There were many African American scouts and spies throughout the Civil War. At the beginning of the Civil War, Allan Pinkerton screened "contrabands", deserters, refugees, and prisoners of war, who entered Union lines.[10] He wrote down the information collected from them. Allan Pinkerton interviewed many African Americans, but was impressed by the intellectual ability of John Scobell, who he employed in the military secret service.[11] Similar to Scobell, Pinkerton was guided by an African American in Memphis, Tennessee when he was suspected by Confederate officials of being a Union follower. A black man by the name of Jem was very helpful in guiding Pinkerton, the chief of the United States Secret Service, in the city of Memphis where he was suspected to be a Union supporter. Jem, a porter in Memphis, behaved like other blacks who worked for the interests of Union soldiers. Upon his knowledge that Confederate spies were monitoring the movement of Allan Pinkerton, Jem did not hesitate to warn him. He informed him that there were many Confederate spies along the river at Cairo spying on the movement of President Lincoln's soldiers. In addition, he told him that one of the spies was following Pinkerton while he was going to his room. The spy who followed Chief Pinkerton seemed to have knowledge about him. In addition, the Confederate spy stipulated to Jem that Pinkerton was suspicious and he had seen him in Cincinnati. When Jem believed that Chief Pinkerton's life was in danger, he procured a horse near the hotel so that the secret service chief would leave the city without delay. Moreover, he guided him safely to the lines and outside the city allowing Chief Pinkerton to escape to safety. After many years, Jem met Chief Pinkerton who employed him in the United States Secret Service. In the service, he strongly proved his devotion.[12]

Similar to Jem, during the war of the rebellion, African Americans voluntarily provided information regarding the rebels to Chief Pinkerton.[13] Even though African slaves were prone to telling Union soldiers about the rebels' movement and other military information few were employed in the United States Secret Service at that time. Many sources mention the name of John Scobell, an operative agent in the service of the United States Secret Service under the jurisdiction of Chief Allan Pinkerton.

John Scobell

John Scobell was a slave who was freed during the Civil War by his master of the same name. He told Allan Pinkerton during his prescreening that he was originally from the state of Mississippi. We know little about his life in Mississippi. He only told Chief Allan Pinkerton that he travelled to Virginia with his master, who was a Scotchman, and taught him his native music. This African American was well accustomed with Scottish music which his master loved to hear. After music training from his master, he mastered the Scottish ballad. John Scobell's wife was freed with him and found employment in Richmond. Unlike him, there is no information about his wife that is worth discussing. Scobell escaped to the Union line where he was received by a guard who introduced him to Pinkerton. After being interviewed by the secret service chief, Mr. Scobell was employed by him to serve as an operative agent in the secret service. It appears that he was the first person of color to be employed in the secret service of the United States. There is no record indicating that before Mr. Scobell, there were any African Americans in that agency.

Allan Pinkerton worked for his private security agency named the Pinkerton National Detective Agency before his entrance into the Secret Service. He was also a good friend of President Abraham Lincoln. Moreover, he was connected to John Brown, who hated the institution of slavery. Allan Pinkerton conducted many Underground Railroad missions to assist black people in escaping to freedom. He became accustomed to African Americans during his underground missions. Pinkerton also utilized the expertise of his force in securing the trip of President Lincoln from Springfield to Philadelphia to Washington, D.C. During the same period, he acted under the direction of the Secretary of War and Colonel Andrew Porter, the provost marshal. In the field, he was under the direct direction of General George B. McClellan.[14] On November 1, 1861, General McClellan was appointed commander in chief of the United States army during the war of the rebellion. After his appointment, he was able to request the service of his former acquaintance to serve as the chief of the Secret Service, an agency he organized the same year he was appointed. The newly organized Secret Service agency was under the jurisdiction of Allan Pinkerton. The management and control of the agency were entrusted to him.[15] According to Allan Pinkerton, General George B. McClellan had a good relationship with him years before the war of the rebellion.[16]

With respect to African Americans, he was probably made familiar with them during his participation in the efforts to free them. There is no question that he might be associated with many black underground conductors and station agents. Possibly, his familiarization with African Americans made it easy for him to communicate with Mr. John Scobell during his interview. Similarly, he was confident that Scobell would serve the Union faithfully and courageously.

In 1861, during his interview with Allan Pinkerton, John Scobell revealed his true character. He was truthful in his responses and described his trip well, and he was identified as an intelligent person by Allan Pinkerton. Due to his demeanor and confidence, Pinkerton referred him to his headquarters with a plan to hire him as a scout. As he went to the headquarters, for two weeks he was employed in various minor important assignments. For these minor assignments, the applicant needed secrecy and loyalty which John Scobell had.[17] After the completion of his first assignments, which were well conducted, Pinkerton found that Scobell was able to write and read. Therefore, Pinkerton decided to send him to Virginia to see whether or not he would accomplish his mission well. His first mission to Virginia was completed with the assistance of Timothy Webster, an experienced operative agent of Pinkerton. With Timothy Webster, they travelled through Centreville, Manassas, and Lower and Upper Accoquan. During this secretive mission, Scobell and Webster spied on Gurley who had a document to transmit from Washington to the Confederate supporters. As these two operative agents followed his movements, Webster established a false relationship with the doctor which made it easy to obtain the package from him easily. After establishing a plausible relationship with the doctor, Webster and Scobell were able to take the document from the doctor. Upon taking the document, John Scobell and Timothy Webster passed it to the president of the Loyal League, who then took it to Washington.[18]

Scobell was well connected with African Americans in Leonards Town. During his operative services, this town became his home due to the relationship he forged with the black people. He also received much support from African American members of the Loyal League of that city which is where he resided with the old Uncle Turner. As a free man, Uncle Turner rendered various services to those who needed his services for a cost. In addition to Uncle Turner, Scobell was also known to Uncle Gallus, an African American who was once employed as a workman by the Confederate army for constructing the fortification around Richmond. The president of the league was also acquainted to Scobell.[19] In addition to Webster, Scobell also served along Mrs. Lawton. While conducting their secret operative mission, Mrs. Lawton identified herself as a Southern lady and Scobell was her servant.[20] Possibly, these identities were employed for work purposes to avoid being detected by the Confederate supporters as well as spies which were plenty in the city of Richmond at the time. In regard to the overall performance of Scobell, Pinkerton clearly credited him as well as Timothy Webster and Pryce Lewis as efficient members of his force. He also noted that "they spent much energy in prosecuting the work that was assigned to them."[21] This account of Pinkerton shows that he was capable of performing his duties in the same manner as his white counterparts. Similarly, the same account reveals that team work among this interracial group was taken into account for the success of the agency.

An unnamed person of African descent, who belonged to Winchester, also completed a very difficult intelligence mission by entering the enemy's line for the collection of important information. This unnamed contraband slave was received by the 3rd Massachusetts regiment while it was stationed on the Upper Potomac according to Charles Carleton Coffin. This African American was intelligent, cautious, shrewd, and loyal. He was assigned with the collection of information on the work of the rebels. He passed several times into the lines of rebels while collecting pertinent information, which was then sent to Washington. For the facilitation of his passage, he was furnished with packages of medicine, needles, threads, and other light articles greatly needed in the South. The materials he carried increased the ease of his passage. When he was asked about the reason for his trip, he always replied "been out to get them for master."[22] In addition to his service to the government, he was an influential man among people of color. He noted to his fellow man to keep quiet and "wait till God should give them deliverance" as noted by Carleton Coffin in 1866.[23] Spying methods utilized by these African Americans were difficult to detect because they were familiarized with the region and also with the behavior of the southern people. Moreover, in the beginning of the war, the Confederates did not believe that African Americans would join the Union. Southern planters often told African Americans to dissociate with the Union to avoid being sold to Cuba.

In Missouri, when the guerillas burnt all the railroad bridges, African Americans gave General Schofield important intelligence which enabled him to bring the perpetrators to justice. Six leaders of the rebels were caught and tried by the court marshal, and were shot thereafter.[24] It is plausible to say that without the assistance of African

American informants, the suspected criminals of the Missouri railroads who burnt the bridges wouldn't be arrested. The arrest of those suspects was a sort of deterrence to the rest of the people of Missouri who hoped to act the same way. Throughout the war, there were possibly many Confederate soldiers and spies who were arrested by the Union with the assistance of African Americans.

James Lawson and Black Bob

James Lawson is an African American who rendered intelligence and spy services to the Union. He was a native of Virginia and a slave of Miss Taylor. This African American has been credited with providing Captain Samuel Magaw with valuable information about the movement of the rebels. After gaining the trust of the captain, Lawson was dispatched on a scout mission to the rebel-built fortification. Entering the Confederate army's fortification was dangerous, but Lawson accomplished his mission faithfully. On one occasion, he was sent to Virginia where he risked his life by passing through an area guarded by Confederate sentinels. Even though the road was risky with rebel fire, Lawson returned safely to his destination. Unlike James Lawson, Bob, an African American leader and preacher, acted as a guide for the Union. He entered the enemy zones.

In Virginia, on the bank of the Potomac, an escaped African American who entered the Union lines "informed the generals that his master was a member of the armed league of the Confederate. He went on to tell them that the armed league concealed a large amount of guns and ammunitions in a swamp preparing a sudden attack on the United States army."[25] The weapons were found when the fugitives were sent to look for it and were captured. The information this escaped slave brought to the Union prevented a sudden ambush of the Union army and saved the lives of the Union Soldiers at that time. George Scott, an African American contraband slave, brought important information to the army after his escape. He told them that Confederate insurgents fortified the outposts of the Great and Little Bethel churches located on the road between Yorktown and Hampton. Scott did not limit his contribution by only giving the intelligence. He acted as a guide to accompany General Winthrop to the area where the fortifications were built by the Confederate rebels. Upon their arrival, General Winthrop was satisfied that General Magruder was well prepared to seize Newport and Hampton.[26]

In addition to submitting information to the army, African Americans also instructed the United States Navy generals on the geography of the areas which they were familiar with. Capt. Quincy A. Gillmore received geographical lessons from a slave. When he was in South Carolina, he learned much about the rivers and creeks between Savannah City and Tybee Island. Brutus, the slave who educated Capt A. Gilmore on the geography of the rivers, made his escape from the rebel lines. He instructed Captain Gilmore that "boats drawing ten feet or less could pass at high tide from one part of the Savannah estuary to another, avoiding confederate guns that commanded a narrow stretch of river."[27] Brutus's statement was given much weight by Captain Gilmore. After verifying his information, he found that Brutus was a reliable informant and relied on him in his missions.[28]

Coastal African American runaway slaves, who served as pilots in the Navy made significant contributions in terms of spying as well as piloting. Due to their familiarity with river life, they were well equipped to guide Navy officials while patrolling the rivers. As early as 1861, runaway African Americans from Savannah, Georgia provided pertinent information regarding the navigation of rivers in the surrounding coast of Georgia. Isaac Tatnell, Brutus, and Cassius, all escaped slaves, gave information about the rivers to Admiral Samuel Francis DuPont.[29] Charles Tatnall's services were valued by Lieutenant Penrod Watmough in 1862. According to Jeffrey W. Bolster, the Lieutenant noted that "the knowledge of Charles Tatnall of the entire inland water course was perfect."[30] It appeared that Charles Tatnall guided the lieutenant in the water highway or gave him the exact description of the inland water. When Hilton Head was occupied by the Union Army and Navy, many African American slaves there escaped with some kind of protection. Being friendly to the Union, males and females were also employed by the United States Navy as cooks, stewards, and guides. They served as guides in many expeditions in South Carolina, Georgia, and Florida.

Unlike other contraband slaves who served the Navy in 1861, in 1862, Union officials received quality information from a former Confederate pilot. Robert Smalls, a trusted Confederate pilot, took the ship *Planter* and submitted it to the Union. This black person brought with him important information in addition to the ship as noted by David Dixon Porter, the author of the *Naval History of the Civil War*. According to Porter, Robert Smalls piloted the *Planters* with the Confederate flag while he was in their controlled zone. As he left the confederate jurisdiction, he replaced the Confederate flag with a white flag until he reached the Union lines. Robert Smalls was not requested by any government officials to pirate the Confederate steamer. He did this based on his own conviction. In the steamer, he transported nine people of his own color, including women and children. Admiral DuPont was impressed by Robert Smalls' act. He said that "he gave much valuable information which only a man of his intelligence can do." He went on to note that "he was the most intelligent slave that he had not yet met."[31] Pirating the steamer was a very risky mission that Robert Smalls undertook. If he was arrested, Confederate officials would punish him severely. His act was patriotic and honorable to his people as well as the federal government. Robert Smalls did not value the trust given to him by the Confederate generals. It appeared that his freedom, that of his family, and fellow African Americans who were kept in bondage weighed more than the favor which he received from Confederate authorities. It is also fair to say that Robert Smalls prepared his mission for a significant amount of time, only waiting for the right opportunity. After surrendering the steamer, *Planter*, Robert Smalls was employed as a pilot by Union officials. He served with them until the end of the war.

African American males were not the only spies and scouts employed by United States government officials. Females of the same race volunteered as nurses or were sometimes employed as spies for the Union. Among people of the African race, Harriet Tubman was employed by the government of the United States as a spy, scout, and nurse. In the same capacity, Susie Taylor also volunteered as a scout and nurse in the South Carolina Native Guard during the Civil War. It appears that Sojourner Truth also served as a spy during the Civil War.

Harriet Tubman

In South Carolina, Harriet Tubman was hired as a spy, scout, and nurse. This tremendous African American woman had a history of conducting risky assignments. Before her government employment, she was part of the "Underground Railroad." She assisted many slaves who escaped from slave states to free states. She was associated with many abolitionists and Underground Railroad conductors. She clandestinely completed assignments while a conductor. But during the Civil War, her spying duties became official. She was employed by General Hunter, an abolitionist Massachusetts general. His letter dated Feb. 19, 1863, stated that Harriet Tubman gained her employment through the recommendation of Gov. John Andrew of Massachusetts.[32] In the same letter, General Hunter referred to her as a valuable woman.[33] The credit which she received from General Hunter is worth discussing because Mrs. Tubman's scout missions were very risky and beneficial to the Union. In addition to her scouting and spying, she helped with motivating African American soldiers to enlist in the regiments of General Higginson. Sometimes she would make jokes and sing for them.

With respect to her scouting missions, she was once asked by General Hunter to go to the Combahee River in a gunboat for a scouting mission. She requested from the general that Col. Montgomery be appointed as the commander of the mission if he wanted her assistance.[34] Without any hesitation, Gen. Hunter appointed Col. Montgomery as the commander of the expedition. In regard to her relationship with the soldiers, Mrs. Harriet Tubman made an important impact on the moral of the "contraband" slaves. Many African American runaway slaves did not want to communicate with generals and other unknown persons because they feared that they would be sent to Cuba as their masters had told them. On the other hand, they trusted Mrs. Harriet Tubman without any reserve. Some of them were possibly aware of her contributions to people of her own color during her involvement with the Underground Railroad. Perhaps, in the force, there were soldiers who knew her personally.

Mrs. Harriet Tubman also completed risky missions during the war. Sometimes she spied across the rebel lines collecting valuable information.[35] Scouting and guiding were also part of her assignments during the Civil War. She acted as a spy and guide under Col. Thomas Wentworth and James Montgomery. She travelled with the United States Army in many expeditions in South Carolina and Florida. Mrs. Tubman was also employed as a nurse in the Colored Hospital at Fort Monroe.[36] During her scout missions, she was given assistants by General Hunter. Among her scout assistants were: Peter Barns, Mott Blake, Sandy Silters, Salomon Gregory, Isaac Hayward, Gabriel Cohen, and George Chrisholm, who were all residents of Beaufort, South Carolina. They were familiar with the land which they scouted.[37] It appears that she commanded these African Americans when spying. Possibly, the assistant spies worked under her supervision.

As for Mrs. Harriet Tubman, her patriotic duties for the United States government were commended by many public officials. Among those who credited her valuable services were: Honorable Seward, Secretary of the State and General James Montgomery, Col. Higginson, Mrs. Gen A. Baird, and Hon. Gerrit Smith. Mrs. Harriet Tubman was known to these people for a long period of time. She was known to William Lloyd Garrison, one of the most ardent abolitionists in the United States, and Charles Summer and Wendell Phillips, both Massachusetts abolitionists and friends of the African race. Both senators worked hard for the causes of African Americans, and were determined to abolish slavery in the entire United States at any cost.

The services performed by people of color during the Civil War were critical for the success of the Union. Southern states were highly populated by people of the African race who were kept in bondage for hundreds of years. They were the first enemy of the institution of slavery, and its abolition was their dream. Union generals probably trusted them because of their dislike of slavery. While some Union soldiers were fighting for the cause of the Union, African Americans fought against the institution of slavery. They were obligated to spy, scout, and in-form Union generals of all the activities of the Confederates. African Americans escaping slavery was psychological warfare to the slave mas-ters. Surely, they were terrified and worried about their lives because they feared revenge from their former slaves. On the other hand, the Union took advantage of the escaped slaves by employing them in the army and as scouts. As African Americans became better at spying, their services were valued and the need of enlisting them increased. Civil War historians did not complain about African American spies; most of them complimented the services they provided for the Union.

Robert Smalls

As previously mentioned, African American spy and scout Robert Smalls executed a courageous naval mission during the Civil War. This African American voluntarily brought out a Confederate steamer by the name *Planter* to the Union line. He worked on the steamer and was familiar to piloting in the water highway. The steamer was used for transportation of Confederate military equipment and personnel and it was under the charge of Brigadier-General Ripley in Charleston, South Carolina.[38] Due to his piloting experience, he was trusted by his superiors. It appears that Confederate officers did not predict Smalls' actions. Due to his courage as well as his patriotism to his country, he was always respected by Union generals and other supporters. During the Reconstruction Period, he held many law enforcement positions. He was born in Beaufort, South Carolina in 1839.[39]

The arming of African slaves at the start of the Civil War was op-posed by Americans throughout the country with some exceptions. On the contrary, their employment as spies and scouts were not chal-lenged by Northern inhabitants and other regions of the United States excepting the states under seccession. Slaves had local knowledge in the South. They were familiar with land and water highways. There-fore, their employment as spies for the Union were necessary. A large number of African Americans voluntarily enlisted as spies and scouts. In this capacity, they entered into the Confederate camps collecting data on their military plans, equipment, and intellignence. In conclusion, the deeds of African American spies contributed largely to the destruction of many planned ambushes against Union soldiers. In addition, Confederate advances were also hampered by Union soldiers through the intelligence collected by spies of both races.

Notes

1 Benson John Lossing, *Pictorial History of the Civil War in the United States of America*, 1866, p.500. There were also African American slaves who acted as pilots and others enlisted in the Confederate Army.

2 John Stevens Cabot Abbott, *The history of the Civil War in America*, vol.1, H. Bill, 1863, pp.136 – 137, 141.

3 William A. Dobok, *Freedom by the Sword: The U.S. Colored Troops, 1862 – 1867*. Army Historical Series, Center of Military History United States Army, Washington, D.C., 2011, p.160.

4 Lafayette Charles Baker, *History of the United States Secret Service*, L.C. Baker, 1867.

5 Allen Pinkerton, *The Spy of the Rebellion: Being a True History of the Spy System of the United States Army during the Late Rebellion*, (G,W) Carleton, 1883, p.245.

6 Ibid.

7 Baker, 1867, p.34.

8 Sarah Emma Evelyn Edmonds, *Nurse and Spy in the Union Army: Comprising the Adventure and Experience of a Woman in Hospital*, Camps, and Battlefield. Subscription only by W.S. Williams & Company, 1865, p.xv.

9 Ibid.

10 Pinkerton, 1833, p.243.

11 Ibid, p,360.

12 Ibid, p.195.

13 Ibid, p.194.

14 Ibid, p.xxvi – xxvii.

15 Ibid, p.245.

16 Ibid, p.153.

17 Ibid, p.345.

18 Ibid, pp.360 – 366.

19 Ibid, p.318.

20 Ibid, p.371.

21 Ibid, p.464.

22 Charles Carleton Coffin: *Four years of Fighting.* Ticknor and Field, 1866, p.43.

23 Ibid.

24 Ibid, p.49.

25 Abott, 1863, p.141.

26 Benson John Lossing, *Pictorial History of the United States,* 1866, pp.503-506.

27 Dobok, 2011, p.29.

28 Ibid.

29 Walter J. Fraser, *Savannah in the Old South.* University of Georgia, 2005, p.329.

30 Jeffrey W. Bolster, *Black Jacks: African American Seamen in Age of Sail,* Harvard University, 2009, p.133.

31 David Dixon Porter, *The Naval History of the Civil War.* Courier Dover Publications, 1886, p.86.

32 Sarah Opkins Brodford, *Scenes in the life of Harriet Tubman*, W.J. Moses, printers, 1869, p.69.

33 Ibid.

34 Ibid, p.39.

35 Ibid.

36 Ibid, p.71.

37 Ibid.

38 David Dixon Porter, *The Naval History of the Civil War.* Courier Dover Publishing, 1886, p.54.

39 Ibid.

CHAPTER VIII

African American Spies in the
Confederate White House

During the War between the States, the Union and the Confederacy used contingents of spies to collect information and military data against each other. According to historians, both sides used spies for the collection of military data. While much of the spying was orchestrated in the war field or in towns, an exeptional feature of spying was conducted inside the White House of the Confederate president in Richmond, Virginia. Similar attempts were also conducted in the White House of the United States government in Washington, D.C., where President Abraham Lincoln resided.

In 1861, with the seccession of Southern states, the political landscape of the American government was shaped. The country was divided into two segments: the Confederate States of America and the United States of America. The Confederate States of America had as its first capital, the city of Montgomery, Alabama. When President Lincoln ordered an attack against the seceded states, the capital of the Confederate States was moved to Richmond, Virginia. As a slave owner, President Davis took with him his faithful free African American body-servants, James H. Jones and Robert Brown.[1]

On the 20th of May, 1861, when President Davis moved to Richmond, Virginia, he resided on the corner of Twelfth and Clay where the White House of the Confederate States was situated. As noted already, he had with him his African American servants. But in Richmond, he also employed a number of African Americans. Historically,

President Davis was accustomed to employing African slaves as his servants for his plantation. He did not mistrust them or believe they were spies. Among the free African Americans who resided in Richmond with the president was the son of his slave, friend and companion, James Pemberton. Robert Brown, a free African American, was the servant of Mrs. Davis. Like Jones, Brown was faithful to the Davis family. While James Jones was the servant of the presdent, Brown was the faithful servant of Mrs. Davis.[2] When the president evacuated from Richmond, Virgina, Brown went with Mrs. Davis and her children from Fortress Moroes to Savannah where they were captured.[3] Brown protected the entire family. Another person worth noting is Ellen, a mulatto, and the maidservant of the president. She was also at the White House of the Confederate States. Little is recorded on Ellen.[4] Another free African American in the Davis family was James Henry Brooks.[5] Little is known about the service performed by this African American in the family of President Jefferson Davis.

On the contrary, African slaves employed in the city of Richmond were given spy missions in the Confederate States of America. Among the African slaves and servants hired for the service of the president was Mary Elizabeth Bowser, an African American woman spy.

Mary Elizabeth Bowser in the Confederate White House

The first known African American spy in the Confederate White House was Mary Elizabeth Bowser. She was employed by a reputed Union supporter and spy during the war, Elizabeth Van Lew. This white woman detested slavery as well as the secession of Southern states. With such convictions, she devoted her time to serve the United States as a spy. She employed many African Americans in her spying strategies. Moreover, she used her own houses as spy stations. Van Lew was from a prominent and prosperous family in Richmond, Virginia. They had mansions and slaves. One of the stations where the spying mission was situated was called the Old Van Lew Mansion. In Virginia, Lew had five secret stations reserved for the spying mission. In these stations, African slaves who served as spies were called "Cipher dispatches." Van Lew was born in 1818 in Virginia.[6]

Bowser did not reject the request to become a spy from her former mistress. Bowser was a slave in the Van Lew family. With the assistance of Van Lew she was emancipated and sent to school in New England. When the Civil War began, she was called by Van Lew to serve her country as a spy. She did not hesitate to take on such a dangerous mission. Before being employed as a maid in the Confederate White House, Bowser received rigourous spy training. It appears that after her training, Van Lew found her employment in the Confederate White House.[7]

It appears as a person of African descent, President Jefferson Davis and his wife did not object her employment. In the Confederate White House a number of African Americans were already employed. During her employment, Bowser collected pertinent information for the Union which she passed down to Van Lew. William Gilmore Beyner states that Bowser heard the conversations of President Davis at the dining table. The information Van Lew received from Bowser was always transmitted to Union officials in Washington and to generals such as Ulysses S. Grant. The information that Bowser collected from the Confederate White House was also sent to General George H. Sharpe, the chief of the Bureau of Military Information.

As stated above, other African Americans worked in the White House of the Confederate States. In addition to the Davis' free African Americans, whom he brought from Montgomery, Alabama, Spencer was hired in Richmond along with Bowser. He was a slave of the Richmond family. It is unknown whether or not Spencer also served as a spy. He was close to the Davis family and always called the president "Marse Jeff."[8] He was assigned with answering the bell at the door. It seems that he was in charge of the entrance to the White House of the Confederate States government. According to Century Magazine, he sometimes denied visitors access to President Davis. When visitors looked for President Davis, he would sometimes state that he was absent from the White House. The magazine also noted that Spencer had a temper. When a visitor frustated him, he would say "I tell you Sir, Marse Jeff clines [declines] to see you."[9] Spencer was very disciplined and strict. When he refused entrance to a visitor, he would not change his position unless there was an intervention from the president's inner circle. Spencer's account is used to show that the enslaved African spy employed by Van Lew did not have difficulties accesssing the Confederate White House. It is unquestionable that Spencer served people of his race. He was known among people of his color and it would be suicidal for him to deny them any request. It was common during this period of time for slaves to support the causes of their race.

African slave spying was not limitted to military activities only. With the help of Union spies, they were utilized as spies in the White House of the Confederate government. Those who served in this scheme were employed as servants for the president's family. African slaves who served as spies in the White House of the Confederate States served the American government with loyalty under the leadership of Van Lew, the spy master in Richmond, Virginia.

Notes

1 See The Sewannee Review Vol.16. "Jefferson Davis, the Negroes and the Negro Problem." University of the South, 1908, p.417.

2 Ibid, p.418.

3 Ibid.

4 The Century: 1883, volume 27, "The Capture of Jefferson Davis. An Extract from a Narrative, writte not published, but for the Entertainment of my children only." Century Company, 1884, p.130.

5 See The Sewannee Review, 1908, p.416.

6 See William Gillmore Beymer, "Miss Van Lew" in Haper's Magazine, vol, 123. Harper's Magazine Foundation, 1911, p.86. See Also Scouts and Spies of the Civil War written by William Gilmore Beyner and published by the University of Nebraska Press, 1912, p.54. Kate Dickinson Sweetser, Ten American Girls from History. Elizabeth Van Lew: The Girl who Risked all that Slavery might be Abolished and the Union Preserved. Harper, 1917, p.86.

7 See Sweetser, 1917, p.101. See also Beyner, 1911, p.90.

8 See "The Capture of Jefferson Davis" in the Century; 1883, vol.27, 1884, p.132.

9 Ibid, p.132.

CHAPTER IX

James H. Jones and Benjamin Montgomery Deeds for President Jefferson Davis

In Chapter VII, I noted that James H. Jones, a free African American, was a body-servant of President Jefferson Davis. According to his own account, he was born in Raleigh, North Carolina. When the president moved to Richmond, Virginia, Jones was also part of the family household who went with the president. While in Richmond, Virginia, Jones was entrusted with important secrets of the Confederate government. He was dispatched with a large amount of money destined to Confederate Captain Parker of South Carolina. In addition to his government duties, he was a valet and coachman for the president. According to Jones, he was once commissioned with a secret mission to deliver a sum of thirteen million dollars in gold and silver coin from Richmond, Virginia. He also said that he had this amount of money for four weeks. He kept the mission secret to any other person except President Davis and Confederate Captain Parker of South Carolina where the money was to be delivered. He said that "when I got it (money) in two trunks, I conveyed it on the railroads as common baggage (although I guarded it) to its destination in Newberry, South Carolina, where I delivered it to Captain Parker."[1] It appears that Jones was dutiful in completing the assignment he was entrusted with.

Jones' Civil War mission was very dangerous. The United States Secret Service employed many agents to spy on Confederate officers and supporters engaging in forgery and money laundering. If caught with such an amount of money, Jones would have been arrested, charged, and imprisoned for a federal crime. It is plausible to argue that Jones was not a Confederate sympathizer. He indirectly assisted the Confederate government due to his loyalty to his master whom he admired. Before the presidency of Jefferson Davis, Jones was his bodyguard. But his messengership was materialized during the administration of President Davis. In 1895, author Edward Austin Johnston recorded that Jones served as "messenger to President Davis of the Confederacy at Richmond, Virginia."[2]

The assignment entrusted to Jones in Richmond indicates that President Davis valued the mental and intellectual capacities of Jones in handling delicate missions. It seems that he believed in him and considered him to be the most trusted person among the African race at the Confederate White House. Like his master, Jones also gave weight to his relationship with his master, President Davis. Even after the fall of Richmond, Jones did not leave his master. They fled together to Georgia where they were arrested. Johnston writes "James H. Jones of Raleigh was caught with him [President Jefferson Davis] by the Union troops in southwest Geargia and was also confined with him in the "Rip-Raps," at Hampton Roads, Virginia."[3] Jones' loyalty to his master was unquestionable. Before the arrest of his master, President Davis, Jones attempted to assist him in escaping from the Union soldiers. He was the first to detect the Union gun fire in the areas where the president was sleeping. In his book, President Davis wrote about the Union gun fire before his capture as follows: "a free colored man who clung to our fortune, came and told me there was firing over the branch."[4] The man of color noted by the president was identified by him as being James Jones. Jones travelled with the president from Danville, Virginia to Georgia where he was captured. After his liberation from the prison, he kept a line of communication with Mrs. Davis, the wife of President Davis.

During the Reconstruction Period, Jones was engaged in local politics in Raleigh, North Carolina. Johnston noted that he was a member of the Board of Aldermen. In 1922, the Negro Year Book recorded that Jones also served as a messenger in the Senate while he was residing in Washington, D.C. Similar to Jones, Benjamin Montgomery also rendered valuable services to President Jefferson Davis and his brother Joe Davis.

Benjamin Montgomery

Similar to Jones at Brierfield, Benjamin Montgomery was the manager of the Hurricane Plantation belonging to Joe Davis, the brother of President Jefferson Davis.[5] Brierfield and Hurricane were thirty miles below Vicksburg, as noted by Morris Schaff.[6] At the Hurricane Plantation, Montgomery received the favor of his master. He was given access to instructions as if he were a free person. According to scholars and historians, his master, Joe Davis, lent him books and other readable materials for his own intellectual development. As such, Montgomery took advantage and learned how to read and write. As a result, he was appointed the manager of the Hurricane Plantation. In this position, it is unknown whether or not he acted as a plantation judge as James Pemberton at the Brierfield Plantation. It is known Joe Davis utilized the same slave self-governing approach as his brother, Jefferson Davis, at his plantation. The management of slaves at the Hurricane Plantation is not the primary objective of this discussion regarding the contributions made by Montgomery to his masters. Montgomery's risky mission for the preservation and safety of his masters from the Union is the most pertinent aspect to discuss.

During the Civl War, Union soldiers were prone to destroying properties held by slave owners, especially those who joined the Confederate government. Similarly, properties of high ranking Confederate officials were also confiscated. On July 17, 1862, the United States Congress passed "an act to supress insurrection, punish treason, and rebellion, seize, and confiscate the property of rebels, and for other purposes." With the passage of this act, the attorney general of the United States was empowered with the right to act in accordance with the act.

Fearing the loss of the plantation of his master's brother and the estate of his master, Montgomery designed a misleading plan for the preservation of his master's properties. Hubert Todd Houston collected authoritative data from the documents in possession of Major J. Coleman Alderson of Charleston, West Virginia.[7] As the First Lieutenant of Company A, 36th Battalion, Virginia Cavalry in the Confederate Army, Major Alderson had access to correspondence with the President Jefferson Davis and other high ranking officials. From his collection, the plans orchestrated by Benjamin Montgomery were revealed.

In 1861, when President Davis moved to Richmond, Virginia, he charged Montgomery with the management of the Brierfield Plantation. Similarly, his brother Joe Davis left Montgomery in charge of his Hurricane Estate when he was commissioned general in the Confederate Army. As a faithful and trusty slave, Montgomery was honored by such responsibility. But with the fall of New Orleans, Montgomery believed that the future of his masters's properties were at risk. In his opinion, the route from New Orleans to Mississippi was accessible. Therefore, he was obliged to design a magnificent strategy to mislead Union officials and President Lincoln of the United States. His first reaction was to travel to Richmond, Virginia, and share his plan with President Jefferson Davis. After careful examination, he put his decision into practice after he met President Jefferson Davis. Upon their first contact, Montgomery explained the danger of losing the plantation to the Union. He suggested that the president should sell the properties to him as a symbolic gesture. After the war, the president and his brother could recuperate their properties. President Davis's answer was not beyond belief. He told Montgomery that he was a slave and he could not sell property to him. But the answer did not please Montgomery who desired to protect the properties of his masters. The plan of Montgomery was as follows:

> "The president and his brother, General Joe Davis, should sell the plantations to him, Bob Montgomery, for which he should execute his notes, covering the full purchase money, and give a deed of trust on the property to secure the payment of the notes, that when the war should be over, there being default in the payment of the notes, the mortgage should be forclosed, and the legal title should repass to the original owners."[8]

When President Davis refused to sell the property to him due to his slave status, Montgomery took a different approach for the same purpose. His next strategy was as follows: "President Davis should first voluntarily grant him freedom and issue a public record for the act of the emancipation."[9] Thereafter, Montgomery would have had a legal way to purchase the estates. The second proposition was sound to President Davis. As a result, he had a meeting with his brother General Joe Davis for the matter in question. After consulting with his brother, the president came to a decision and the documentation for the liberation of Montgomery from slavery was issued and he became a free man. As a free man, he could legally own properties in the state of Mississippi.[10]

Upon receiving his deed of emancipation, Montgomery returned to Mississippi and authenticated his certificate of emancipation. Records for the document were submitted to the state government. The next plan for Montgomery was to seek protection from the government of the United States. He was aware that Union soldiers would not protect the plantation without a legal document from high-ranking Union officials. He went to Washington and presented to President Lincoln his certificate of emancipation as well as his land deed. He expressed to the president that Jefferson Davis sold him his plantation. But fearing the destruction from the Union, he wanted his support for the protection of his newly purchassed land. As the plantation of Brierfield was popularly known as belonging to President Jefferson, the risk of its destruction was high. Similarly, the estate of Hurricane was also in the same status. His request from President Lincoln was accepted and an official document was prepared for him. The order issued by President Lincoln declared that Union officials or military would not destroy or damage the plantations of Brierfield and Hurricane belonging to Benjamin Montgomery, a free man of the United States. Montgomery published his offical order for the protection of his plantations among the army. As a result, no military men, companies, squads, or individual harrased him for holding the plantations which belonged to President Davis and his brother.[11]

Montgomery kept his design and at the close of the war, President Davis and his brother Joe Davis recuperated their properties from him. As noted above, the mortgage was forclosed due to payment default. Montgomery's plan is classified as intelligence service. If caught, he would have been charged as a supporter of the Confederate government. Montgomery was loyal to his masters. Even though the first plan was orchestrated for the misleading of Union officials, President Davis and his brother did sell the plantations to Montgomery and his sons after awhile. The account noted by Varina Davis reveals the transactions made by the Montgomery family for the purchase of the Brierfield and Hurricane plantations. She noted that after the war, the Montgomery family purchased our two plantations, "the Hurricane" and the "Brierfield."[12] It seems that many planters wanted to buy those plantations, but the Davis' family preferred to sell it to their former slaves. According to Mrs. Davis, the Montgomery family paid $300,000 for the property.[13] Benjamin Montgomery was a wealthy man from the plantation. Mrs. Davis wrote that he owned a shop and purchased fruit crops for the Davis families. Likely, he bought crops from other people in "the Bend".[14] At one time, "he credited one of the Davis's family $2,000 on his account."[15] Just as any business person, Montgomery sometimes borrowed from his master and honored his debts accordingly.[16] Benjamin Montgomery had two sons, Thorton and Isaiah. As an instructor, Montgomery instructed his children in the art of reading and writing. As educated men, they became responsible people as noted by the president's wife.[17]

Isaiah Montgomery's legacy continued for many years. The skills he acquired from the "Davis Bends" were put into action when he built the town of Mount Bayou. In Mount Bayou, he utilized the same legal proceedings as at the Hurricane and Brierfield Plantations. Democratic norms were observed faithfully. Law and order were also enforced impartially. His contributions to the improvement of Mount Bayou was credited by missionaries, government officials, and African American leaders such as Booker T. Washington. Before the establishment of Mount Bayou, Isaiah Montgomery was one the Mississippi convention delegates for the amendment of the Constitution which disenfranchised African Americans in 1890.

Jones and Montgomery were faifthul servants and friends of the Davis family. These two individuals served their masters with loyalty and unconditional love and respect. Even after their separation, they communicated with their former masters. Like these two Africans, the Davis family also honored their relationship with their former slaves. They trusted them as well and believed in their progress.

Notes

1   Charles Roman, *The Scrop Book. A Secret of the Confederacy. Entrusted with the Seal of the Southern State*, A Negro Declares that the knowledge of its local shall die with him. Frank A. Munsey, 1908, p.228.

2   Edward Austin Johnston, *A School History of the Negro Race in America from 1619 to 1890, With a Short Introduction as to the origin of the Race: Also a Short Sketch of Liberia*. W,B. Conkey Company, 1895, p.136.

3   Ibid, p.137.

4   See Varina Davis, Jefferson Davis. *Ex-President of the Confederate States of America. A Memoire by His Wife in two volumes*. New York, Belford Company, Publishers, 1891, p.638.

5   Booker T. Washington, *The Story of the Negro: The Rise of the Race from Slavery* vol.1. Doubleday, Page, Company, 1909. Washington writes that Montgomery supervised the Hurricane plantation of Joseph Emory Davis. He went on to relate that Montgomery had a fair education.

6   Morris Schaff, Jefferson Davis: His Life and Peronality. J.W. Luce, 1922, 1922, p.26.

7   Hubert Todd Houston, "Bob Montgomery." The American Magazine, vol.82. Crowell-Collier Publisher Company, 1916, p.112.

8   Ibid, 1916, p.112.

9   Ibid.

10 Ibid.

11 Ibid.

12 Ibid.

13 Davis, 1890, p.175.

14 Ibid.

15 Ibid.

16 Ibid, p.174.

17 Ibid, 175.

CHAPTER X

The Scouting and Spying
of Dabney and George Scott

During the Civil War, African Americans, free and slaves, voluntarily assisted the Union with military intelligence information. Similarly, they guided the Union army and spies into the Confederate lines. Even though a large number of African Americans served as such, at the start of war, few contraband slaves pleased Union generals in terms of the details and descriptions of the enemies and the opportunities to inflict major destructions on the Union regiments. Among African Americans credited by Union generals were Dabney and George Scott, both contraband slaves.

Dabney, the African American Scout

During the Civil War, many African Americans served as scouts and spies, but records do not reveal that they were engaged in decoding the message of Conderate sympathizers or followers. On the contrary, Dabney was credited with impeccable knowledge on the folkways of Southern planters. Frank Moore, the author of *The Civil War and Story: 1860-1865*, indicates that Dabney was an intelligent African slave. According to Moore, he was a slave who was advertised for sale as a "smart, likely Negro fellow."[1] This indicates that Dabney was intelligent and prudent when compared to other African slaves. Before the war, Dabney resided with his master on the south bank of the Rappahannock not far from Fredericksburg. Upon his escape as a contraband slave during the war, he was discovered by General

Joseph Hooker. It seems that after being interviewed by the general, he proved to be knowledgeable of the region where he lived. Possibly, due to his social and geographical knowledge, the general did not send him away. Instead, he welcomed him to the Union line and became his guide. There is no doubt that after questioning him about his geographical information, Dabney revealed reliable and verifiable information on the county and its inhabitants which seemed important to the general.

Dabney's war contributions were noted by historian Frank Moore. He writes, on one occasison, just before the Battle of Chancellorsville, scouting men from the rebel area reported to the Union officials that the locality where they intended to go was free from Confederate soldiers. According to them, one of the farmers in that area told them "that there were no Southerners anywhere near him, and had not been for several days."[2] Upon listening to the reports of the scouts, Dabney intervened immediately and noted that he knew the planter who informed them about the rebel's locality. He disagreed with the account of the scouts. Without delay, he stated to the general that "you must take him [planter] just contrawise from what he talks." He also pointed out that "if he says there are no rebs there, you may be sure there are plenty of them all about and got their big guns all ready."[3] Even though Dabney's interpretation of the coded words of the planter was well defined, the account of the scouts was believable. When the Union forces were dispatched in the same locality where the planter noted that no rebels were around, they were attacked suddenly upon their arrival in the near neighborhood. They were attacked ferociously and Union soldiers were dispersed throughout the whole area. From thence, the account of Dabney was always taken into account by the Union military officers. After the enemy's attack, Dabney noted that "I know that man very well, he kept saying. "He's my ole [old] masts'r [master] and he's a man you have to take just contrary to what he says."[4]

The analysis of the African slave shows how much they were entrusted by the people who directed their behavior. Due to his knowledge of the Southern folk ways, he was employed as a pilot during scouting. It appears that he was also armed during his service with the Union army. Like Dabney, George Scott, an African slave, also rendered important services to the Union.

George Scott

George Scott is the first African slave who reached Union lines in Virginia. Historians label him as the first contraband slave of the Civil War. During his escape to the Union line, he reported significant information on the location of rebels near Fortress Monroe. James Parton, the author who wrote about General Butler's military duties in New Orleans, credited Scott for his revelations on the rebels. According to Parton, Major Wintrop was advised by Scott that rebels occupied two points between Yorktown and Hampton, where their troops were entrenched. Rebel troops were seizing and plundering the areas where they were stationed. Scott did not mention goods seized or plundered by rebels. The locations where rebels were stationed proved to be correct. Due to such mastery, General Whintrop employed him as a guide. His assessments on the rebels were always verifiable except in one occasion when he was inaccurate as noted by Parton.[5] From the account of Benson John Lossing, data showed that George Scott informed Union gererals that the rebels fortified the outpost at Great and Little Bethel Church preparing to attack Union forces on the road between Yorktown and Hampton and thereafter confined General Buttler at Fort Monroe.[6]

Notes

1 Frank Moore, *Anedoctes, Poetry and Incidents of the War, North and South, 1860-1865,* 1867, pp.268-269.

2 Ibid.

3 Ibid.

4 Ibid.

5 James Parton, *General Butler in New Orleans.* Mason Brothers, 1864, p.140.

6 Benson John Lossing, *The Pictorial Book of the Civil War in the United States of America,* vol.1. T. Belknap, 1874, pp.500-504.

CHAPTER XI

Conclusion and Summary

The employment of African Americans has a long history in the United States. From this research, data indicates that an African American was appointed justice of the peace in Newmarket, New Hampshire during the colonial era. This same person continued to serve as a law enforcement officer in the same city in different capacities. In the same region, African Americans served as justices of peace in Massachusetts. As in Massachusetts, in Ohio, another African American served in the city council. African Americans employed in law enforcement in the New England region were educated and capable of performing the duties entrusted to them. The same conditions that applied in Ohio also applies to California where another African American was also elected to the city council. African Americans were also included in law enforcement in Louisiana.

Historical data reveals that African Americans entrance in law enforcement can be traced to the colonial era. During William C.C. Claiborne's governership of Louisiana, African Americans were empowered with police and militia duties. Even though they served as such, in the 1820's they were prohibited from performing law enforcement duties. Data shows that before the Civil War, African Americans were enlisted in the militia. But during the Civil War, military officials entrusted them with military police duties. In like manner, in the settlements or villages organized for them by Union soliders, they were privileged with the performance of law enforcement duties for the control of people of their race.

This study does not document all law enforcement positions held by African descendants. Data on this subject is scarce. It is known that some people of the African race could pass for white, but it is unknown whether or not in Southern states such mulattoes were employed as law enforcment anywhere excepting Louisiana. Therefore, more objective research is needed to bring to light overlooked law enforcement duties performed by African Americans who could be identified as white during the period under investigation.

BIBLIOGRAPHY

PRIMARY SOURCES

Civil War

Hewett, Jones B., Supplement to the Official Records of the Union and Confederate Armies, vol. 78. Series No.90. Wilmington, N.C., Broadfoot Publishing Company, 1998.

Hewett, Janet B., Supplement to the Official Records of the Union and Confederate Armies. Part II. Record of Events vol.27. US Colored Troops. Wilmington, N.C.: Boadfoot Publishing, 1998

National Archives & Records Administration Featured Documents. The Emancipation Proclamation January 1, 1863.

National Archives, Teaching with Documents: The Fifth for Equal Rights: Black Soldiers in the Civil War. Preserving the Legacy of the United States Colored Troops.

The Civil War Archives. Union Regimental Histories. United States Colored Troops Infantry.

The War of the Rebellion: A Compilation of the Official Records of the Union and Confederate Armies, Washington City, January, 26, 1863. U.S. Government Printing Office, 1899.

Louisiana Militia And Police

Louisiana Department of Culture, Recreation and Tourism. Louisiana Two Century Laws. History of the Battle of New Orleans.

The Louisiana Digest. Louisiana Supreme Court, Acts on Free People of Color, B.Levy, 1841.

PRIMARY AND SECONDARY SOURCES (Book Form)

Anderson, Eric, *Race and Politics in North Carolina, 1872-1901: The Black Second.* Baton Rouge: LSU Press, 1981.

Armistead, Wilson, *A Tribute for the Negro.* Negro University Press, 1848.

Bradford, Sarah O., *Scenes in the Life of Harriet Tubman.* W.J. Moses, Printers, 1869.

Brown, William W., *The Negro in the American Rebellion: His Heroism and His Fidelity.* Lee & Shepard, 1867.

Burges, John W., *The Civil War and the Constitution, 1859-1865,* vol.2. C. Scribner's Sons, 1901.

Butterfield, Daniel, *Major-General Joseph Hooker and the Troops from the Army of the Potomac at Wauhatchie, Lookout Mountain and Chattanooga.* Exchange Printing Company, 1896.

Coffin, Charles C., *Four Years of Fighting.* Ticknor and Fields, 1866.

Cox, Samuel S., *Union-Disunion-Reunion. Three Decates of Federal Legislation.* Punan Knoccuk, 1904.

Danning, William A., *Reconstruction, Political and Economic, 1865-1877,* vol.22. Harper & Brothers, 1877.

Douglass, Frederick, *My Bondage and my Freedom.* Miller, Orton & Mulligan, 1855.

Du Bois, W.E.B., *Black Reconstruction in America 1860-1880.* Simon and Schuster, 1935.

Ducan, Russell, *Freedom's Shore: Tunis Campbell and the Georgia Freedmen.* University of Georgia Press, 1986.

Dulaney, Marvin W., *Black Police in America.* Indiana University Press, 1996.

Downing, Alexander G., *Downing's Civil War Diary.* Historical Department of Iowa, 1916.

Emilio, Luis F., *History of the Fifty-Four Regiment of Massachusetts Volunteer Infantry, 1863-1865.* Boston Book Company, 1894.

Fertig, James W., *The Secession and the reconstruction of Tennessee.* The University of Chicago Press, 1898.

Fleming, Walter L., *Documentary History of Reconstruction, Political,*

Military, Social, Religious, Educational & Industrial, 1865 to the Present Time, vol.2. A.H. Clark Company, 1907.

Fleming, Walter L., *Civil War and Reconstruction in Alabama.* Columbia University Press, 1905.

Fortier, Alicee, *History of Louisiana*, vol.4. Goupil & Company of Paris, 1904.

Garner, James W. *Reconstruction in Mississippi.* Macmillan, 1902.

Gayarre, Charles, *History of Louisiana.* F.F. Hansell & Bro, Ltd. Pelican Printing, 1999.

Greeley, Horace, *The American Conflict: A History of the Great Rebellion in the United States of America, 1860-65.* O.D. Case, 1867.

Hamilton, Joseph Gregoire de R., *Reconstruction in North Carolina.* Columbia University, 1914.

Harden, William, *A History of Savannah and South Georgia,* vol.2. Lewis Publishing Company, 1913.

Hazelton, Joseph P., *Scouts, Spies, and Heroes of the Great Civil War.* Providence, R.I. W.W. Thompson & Co., 1893.

Higginson, Thomas W., *Army Life in a Black Regiment.* Boston: Field, Osgood, & Co., 1870.

Hurd, John C., *The Law of Freedom and Bondage in the United States,* vol.2. Little, Brown, 1862.

Jackson, Luther P., *Negro Office Holders in Virginia, 1865-1895.* Norfolk, Guide Press, 1945.

James, A.R., *Standard History of Memphis, Tennessee: From a Study of the Original Sources.* H.W. Crew, 1912.

Johnson, Edward A., *History of Negro Soldiers in the Spanish American War: And other Items of Interest.* Capital Printing Company, 1899.

Keating, John M. and Vedder, O.F., *History of the City of Memphis and Shelby County, Tennessee: With Illustrations and Biographical Sketches of some of its Prominent Citizens,* vol.1 D. Mason & Company, 1888.

King, Grace E., New Orleans: *The Place and the People.* Macmillan, 1896.

Knox, Thomas W. *Camp-Fire and Cotton-Field: Southern Adventure in Time of War.* Blelock and Company, 1865.

Langston, John M., *From the Virginia Plantation to the National Capital, Or, The Only Negro Representative In Congress, from the Old Dominion,* Arno Press, 1894.

Latour, Arsene L., *Historical Memoir of the War in West Florida and Louisiana in 1814 -15.* With Atlas. John Conrad and Company, 1816.

Lossing, Benson J., *Pictorial History of the Civil War in the United States of America,* J. H. Butler & Company, 1874.

Martin, Francois-Xavier, *The History of Louisiana.* Printed by Lyman and Beards Lee, 1827.

McPherson, James M., *The Struggle for Equality: Abolitionists and the Negro in the Civil War and Reconstruction.* Princeton University Press, 1867.

Moore, Frank, *Anedoctes, Poetry and Incidents of the War, North and South, 1860-1865,* Publisher not mentioned, 1867.

Nell, William C., *The Colored Patriots of the American Revolution.* Robert F. Walcut, 1855.

Nordhoff, Charles, *The Cotton States in the Spring and Summer of 1875.* B. Franklin, 1876.

Oberholtzer, Ellis P., *A History of the United States Since the Civil War,* vol.1. MaCmillan, 1917.

Parton, James, *General Butler in New Orleans.* Mason Brothers, 1864.

Peters, Madison C., *The Distribution of Patriotism in the United States. Patriotic League,* 1913.

Phillips, Ulrich B., American Slavery: *A Survey of the Supply, Employment and Control of Negro Labor as Determined by the Plantation Regime.* rpr. Baton Rouge, 1966.

Pinkerton, Allen, *The Spy of the Rebellion: Being a True History of the Spy System of the United States Army During the Late Rebellion Revealing many Secrets of the War Hitherto not Made Public.* G.W. Carleton, 1886.

Porter, David D., *The Naval History of the Civil War.* Courier Dover Publications, 1886.

Quarles, Benjamin, *The Negro in the Civil War.* Da Capo Press, 1953.

Reid, Whitelaw, *After the War: A Southern Tour: May 1, 1865, to May 1, 1866.* Moore. Wistach & Baldwin, 1866.

Reilly, Robinson, *The British at the Gate.* The New Orleans Campaign in the War of 1812. G.P. Putnam's Sons. New York, 1974.

Resdunes, Rodolphe L., *Our People and Our History. Fifty Creole Portraits.* LSU Press, 1973.

Reynolds, John S., *Reconstruction in South Carolina, 1865-1877.* Columbia, S.C.: The State Co., 1905.

Richardson, Albert D., *A Personal History of Ulysses S. Grant.* American Publishing Company, 1868.

Rightor, Henry, *Standard History of New Orleans, Louisiana.* Lewis Publishing Company, 1900.

Rowland, Dunbar, *Official Letter Books of W.CC. Claiborne 1801-1816*, vol.2. State Archives and History, 1917.

Satcher, Buford, *Blacks in Mississippi Politics 1865 -1900.* University Press of America, 1978.

Smith, Zachariah F., *The Battle of New Orleans: Including the Previous Engagements between the Americans and the British, the Indians, and the Spanish which led to the Final Conflict on the 8th, Jan, 1815.* J.P. Boston, 1904.

Sterkx, H.E., *The Free Negro in Ante- Bellum Louisiana.* Cranbury, New Jersey: Associated University Press, Inc. 1972.

Taylor, Susie K., *Reminiscences of my Life in Camp with the 33d United States Colored Troops Late 1st S.C. Volunteers.* Boston, published by the author, 1902.

Trowbridge, John T., *The South: A Tour of its Battlefields.* L. Stebbins, 1866.

Wilson, Joseph T., *The Black Phalanx.* American Publishing Company, 1890.

Woodson, Carter G., *Negro Makers of History.* Wildside Press, 2008.

INDEX

Abbott, John Stevens Cabor, 73, 89, 91

Abolitionists, 34, 45, 71, 73
  on employment of African Americans, 121

Act of 1812, 14

Act of 1815, 15

African American regiments. *See also* by specific number
  assumption of patriotic duties by, 74
  formation of, 43, 48, 54, 72–73, 121
  payment of soldiers in, 74

African Americans. *See also* Slaves
  abolitionist generals on employment of, in the Union Army, 121
  arming of, 70, 110, 133–134
  belief in own liberation, 47–48
  at Brierfield and Hurricane plantations, 22–23
  capacities of, in the Union, 56
  in Civil War, xiii–xiv
  as Confederate prisoners-of-war, 74
  for construction of fortification in Confederate areas, 120
  Dabney as scout, 147–149
  dislike for institution of slavery, 53
  Emancipation Proclamation and the employment of, 42–56
  emergency services and, 87–88
  enlistment of, 70
  entrance into Union lines, 44
  in escort services, 90
  exclusion from Union lines, 46
  franchisement of, 34
  in guarding government and private property, 99–102
  in guarding prisoners of war, 62–63, 90–94
  in Hampton, Virginia, 116
  impact of Civil War on lives of, 110
  jail services after the war, 98–99
  as jurymen, 25–26
  law and order in Civil War settlements and villages, 110–118
  in law enforcement
    during the Civil War, 62–102
    before the Civil War in the Northern states, 31–39
    exclusion from duties in peace time, 28, 29
  in law enforcement in Louisiana, 1, 4–16, 102
  liberation of, 43–44
  loyalty to Union, 47, 111
  maintenance of law and order in the plantations before the Civil War, 20–29
  in making arrests, 88–90
  as militiamen before the Civil War in Tennessee and Mississippi Territory, 1–4
  motivation to join the Union army, 48
  need for Union protection, 82
  as officers of the plantation court, 25
  in patrol services, 80–87
  perception of Fleming, Walter L. on court officials as, 26–27
  in prison camp at Morris Island, 94–98
  prison duties performed by, in Civil War, xvi
  protection of, in army camps, 110

African Americans (*continued*)
quelling of slave disorders by, 5
rejection of half pay by, 74
relationships of free, with Claiborne,
William C.. in New Orleans, 5
in setting battery for the rebels, 120
slave status of, in the Constitution, 1
as spies, scouts, and informants in the
Civil War, 120–134, 136–139,
147–149
Stanton, Edwin, on importance of
assistance from, 120–121
as Union spies, 147–149
value of education to, 114
War Department authorization of
regiment of volunteer labors, 48
in War of 1812, xiii, xiv
Alabama. *See also* Montgomery, Alabama, as
first capital of the Confederate States
African American population in, 82
black soldier policing in, 81, 82
Alderson, J. Coleman, 142–143
Alfred (nigger), as servant in Mississippi
Militia, 3
Allegre, Charle, service in law enforcement
by, 9
Allen, Macon Bolling, as justice of the
peace, 37
Allston, Sam, 115
American Antiquarian Society, 31
An Analysis of the Laws of England
(Blackstone), 39
Andrew, John A. (governor of
Massachusetts), 38, 45, 72, 131
enlistment of African Americans and,
73–74
permission to form regiment of people
of color, 53
Arming of African Americans, 70, 110,
133–134
Armistead, Wilson, 37, 38–39
Arrests, making, 88–90
Ashley, James M., on abolition of slavery
and, 56

Bailey, Daniel, defense of Fort Mims by, 3
Bailey, Dixon, defense of Fort Mims by,
2–3

Baird, Mrs. Gen A., on value of Tubman,
Harriet, 132
Baker, Lafayette Charles
as chief of the Bureau of the National
Detective Police, 121–122
on employment of spies, 121
on spying and scouting during Civil
War and, 121, 122
Balkanization, 81
Banks, Nathaniel, formation of regiments
of people of color and, 54
Barns, Peter, as scout assistant to Tubman,
Harriet, 132
Bayne, Thomas, election to city council in
New Bedford, Massachusetts, 36
Beach Branch, South Carolina, 87
Beaufort, South Carolina
African Americans in, 85
Oak Point Plantation in, 79
26th US Colored Infantry at, 87
Belknap, Jeremy, 31
Bellechasse, J.D. de Goutin, militia force
commanded by, 10
Benham, H. W., 70
Benjamin, Judah P., as Confederate
Attorney General, 67
Benjamin (niger), as servant in Mississippi
Militia, 3
Beyner, William Gilmore, 138
Bienville, Jean-Baptiste Le Moyne de,
African American military men
under, 4–5
Bill Hill, Tennessee, 101
Black code laws, 34
Black Reconstruction in America (Du Bois), 6
Blacks. *See* African Americans
The Blacks in Gold Rush California (Lapp),
35
Blackstone, Sir William, 20, 3839
Blake, Mott, as scout assistant to Tubman,
Harriet, 132
Bolen, Augustus, 13
Bolster, Jeffrey, on Tatnall, Isaac, as
information source, 129
Bore, Etienne de, appointment as mayor of
New Orleans, 11
Boute Station, 82
Bowser, Mary Elizabeth, as spy, 137–139

Brierfield plantation, 22
 administration of criminal justice on, 23
 African American law enforcement
  officers at, 22–23
 corrections at, 26
 jury system at, 26
 Pemberton, James, as plantation
  manager at, 29, 142
 Pemberton, James, as presiding judge of
  the plantation court in, 25
 purchase of by Montgomery plantation,
  145
Briggs, George N., 37
Brock, Robert Alonzo, 63, 64
Brooks, James Henry, employment by
  Davis, Jefferson, 137
Brown, John, 125
Brown, Robert, employment by Davis,
  Jefferson, as servant, 136
Brown, William Wells, 38, 53, 78
Brutus (slave)
 education of Gillmore, Quincy A.,
  by, 129
 information provided to Union army
  by, 129
Buford, N. B., 101
Bureau of Colored Regiments, 54
Bureau of Military Information, Sharpe,
  George H. as chief of, 138
Bureau of the National Detective Police
 Baker, Lafayette as chief of, 121–122
 establishment of, to collect intelligence,
  121–122
Burns, Anthony, 37–38
Butler, Benjamin, 47
 confinement of, at Fort Monroe, 149
 freeing of slaves by, 42, 55, 56
 on getting Massachusetts militia ready,
  72
 internationalization of war and, 68
 military duties in New Orleans, 149
 Patton, James, on, 115–116
 policies on escaped slaves, 120
 use of contraband and, 68, 70, 114
 welcoming of runaway slaves by, 120
Butler, Douglass C., 39
Byfield, Massachusetts, Dummer Academy
  in, 31

Cameron, Simon, 42
Campbell, Tunis G., as Freedmen Bureau
  agent, 116–117
Camp Pickering, establishment near
  Memphis, 84
Carey, John L., 68
Carpenter, Francis Bicknell, 50
Casey, Powell A., 10, 13
Cashman, James, as military recruiter, 71
Cassius, information provided to Union
  army by, 129
*Catalogue of Officers and Students
  of Middlebury College in
  Middlebury, Vermont*, 35–36
Cato, Jack, as drummer in War of 1812, 3
Chancellorsville, Battle of, 148
Charleston, South Carolina
 burning of, by rebels, 87–88
 fall of (1865), 86, 89
 prisoner exchange at, 92
Chattanooga, Tennessee
 contraband in, 114–116
 railroads in, 99
Cheswell, Hopestill, 33
Cheswell, Mary Davis, 33
Cheswell, Richard, 33
Cheswell, Thomas, as minister, 33
Cheswell, Wentworth
 as assessor, 32
 attendance at Dummer Academy, 31
 as auditor, 32
 as coroner, 31
 death of, 33
 as judge in the trial of causes, 32
 as justice of the peace in Newmarket,
  New Hampshire, xv, 32
 law enforcement duties of, xvi
 legacy of, 33
 as moderator, 32
 as selectman, 32–33
Chrisholm, George, as scout assistant to
  Tubman, Harriet, 132
Christian, Christopher, as free African
  American militiamen in War of
  1812, 2
Churz, Carl, on Africans as social slaves,
  55–56
"Cipher dispatches," 137

Civil Rights Bill, 53
Civil war, 65–66
Civil War
 African Americans in, xiii–xiv
 Constitution of the United States and,
  65–67
 dual status of, 69–70
 enrollment of African Americans in
  militia before, 1–4
 human intelligence as instrument of, 120
 impact of, on African American lives,
  110
 law enforcement duties of African
  Americans in, xvi
  in the Northern states, 31–39
 liberation of slaves as strategy to weaken
  rebels in, 48
 Lincoln on purpose of, 45, 71
 preservation of Union as sole reason
  for, 47
 prison duties performed by African
  Americans in, xvi
 spying and scouting during, 121
The Civil War and Story, 1860-1865
 (More), 147
Claiborne, William C. C.
 on African Americans' rebellious
  behavior in Louisiana, 10
 concerns over security of New Orleans, 8
 establishment of New Orleans City
  Guard by, 12–13
 on formation of militia force, 14
 as governor of Louisiana and
  Mississippi, 4–5, 17n7
 inclusion policy in the militia under, 7
 on militia training for free African
  Americans, 5
 on regulation of militia of the Territory
  of Orleans, 11, 12
 relationships with influential free
  African Americans in New
  Orleans, 5
Coffin, Charles Carleton, 114
 on African American spying, 127
Cohen, Gabriel, as scout assistant to
 Tubman, Harriet, 132
Coke, Sir Edward, 39
Confederate States of America

arguments supporting existence of,
  66–67
 cabinet officers of, 67
 constitution of, 66–67
 Davis, Jefferson, as president of, 66–67
 Davis, Jefferson's perspective of, 66
 dissertion of soldiers from, 68
 escaped slaves as source of information
  on, 120
 government of, as illegitimate, 69
 lack of legal effect of Constitution of the
  US on, 81
 question of, on legitimacy of, 69
 reasons for fighting Civil War, 65–67
 statehood claim for, 68
 treatment of Union soldiers as invaders,
  81
 Union occupation of, 68
Constables
 selection of slaves as, 23–24
 title of, as antiquated, 24–25
Constitution of the United States. See also
 Law of Nations
 Butler's view of Virginia under, 68
 fighting of Civil War and, 65–67
 lack of legal effect on inhabitants ot the
  Confederate States of America, 81
 lack of status of African Americans in, 1
Contraband
 Butler, Benjamin's use of, as term, 68
 in Chattanooga, 114–116
 compensation of, 42–43
 escaped African Americans as, 70
 escape of Dabney as, during war,
  147–148
 identification of slaves as, 42, 43
 treatment of escaped, 69
 Tubman's impact on moral of, 131–132
Corinth, Mississippi, 55th United States
 Colored Infantry at, 101
Corrections, employment of African slaves
 in, 26
Cuffee, Paul, 36

Dabney
 as African American scout, 147–149
 geographical knowledge of, 148
 reliability of, 148

Darien, Campbell, settlement in Tunnis, 117
Davis, Isaac, 23
Davis, Jefferson, 22, 23
  in the administration of punishment
    and, 27
  as Colonel of the 1st Mississippi Rifles,
    28
  employment of African American
    servants by, 28–29, 136–137
  Jones, James H., as servant of, 140–146
  move to Richmond, 136–137, 140, 143
  Pemberton, James, and, 28–29
  perspective of Confederate States of
    America, 66
  power to pardon, 27
  practice of impartial justice by, 26
  as president of the Confederacy, 66–67
  recoup of property at close of war,
    144–145
  return to Brierfield from military
    service, 27–28
  sale of property to Montgomery, 143–
    14, 145
  selection of African Americans as
    administrators of the plantation
    court, 25
  selection of African slaves as sheriffs and
    constables, 23–24
  use of slave self-governing approach, 142
  writings of, 141
Davis, Joseph E. (Joe), 22–23, 29
  as lawyer, 23
  recoup of property at close of war,
    144–145
  sale of property to Montgomery, 145
  use of slave self-governing approach, 142
Davis, Varina, 22–23, 145
"Davis Bends," 145
Dearborn, Henry
  establishment of New Orleans City
    Guard and, 12–13
  as Secretary of War, 6, 7, 8–9, 11
De La Croix, Jules, 70
Detention centers, establishment of, 89–90
Dix, John Adams, 45
Dobak, William A., 78
Dodge, M. Grenville, 100
Douglass, Frederick, 20–21, 73

advocation for inclusion of African
    Americans for the cause of the
    Union, 48
  concerns over payment of black soldiers,
    74
  introduction to Lincoln and Stanton, 74
Draper, Alonzo G., 63
Du Bois, W. E. B., 6, 116–117
Dubourg, Pierre Francois, 13
Dulaney, Marvin W., xv–xvi, 9, 11–12,
    13, 39
Dummer Academy (Byfield, MA), 31
DuPont, Samuel Francis
  provision of information on rivers to,
    129
  Small, Robert, and, 130
Durham, Walter T., 84
Duyckinck, Evert Augustus, 85

East Tennessee and Virginia Railroad, 99
Edmonds, Sarah Emma Evelyn, on
    scouting by volunteers during the
    Civil War, 121, 122–123
Education, of African Americans in
    Mitchelville, 114
Edward, Colonel, 21
18th United States Colored Infantry, 76
81st United States Colored Infantry, 101
89th United States Colored Infantry,
    101–102
11th United States Colored Infantry,
    75–76
Ellen (mulatto), move with Davis family,
    137
Emancipation Proclamation, employment
    of African Americans and, 42–56
Emergency services, 87–88
Emilio, Luis Fenollosa, 91
  as captain with the 54th Massachusetts
    black regiment, 62–63, 73, 77, 78,
    86, 89, 90, 93, 94
  as writer, 78, 96
Equality before the law, 38
Escaped slaves
  Butler's policies on, 120
  difficulties of managing the affairs of, 47
  as source of information on the
    Confederacy, 120

Escaped slaves (*continued*)
    as Union assets, 120
Escort services by colored troops, 90

Fairchild, James H., 34
Farmer, John, 31
Females, as spies and scouts, 130–133
15th Regiment, United Statues Colored
    Infantry, 73, 76
5th Massachusetts Colored Cavalry, 75
    guarding of prisoners at Point Lookout,
        Maryland, by, 93
5th New Hampshire Infantry, 63
50th United States Colored Infantry,
    84–85
55th United States Colored Infantry, 76,
    101
54th Massachusetts black regiment
    Emilio, Luis Fenollosa as captain with,
        62–63, 73, 77, 86, 90, 92–94
    formation of, 53, 72
    guarding of prisoners of war at Morris
        Island, 64, 91
    law enforcement duties of, 76
    patrol services and, 86
    police work and, 83
    Shaw, Robert Gould, as commander of, 73
56th United States Infantry, 101
1st Kansas Colored regiment, 83
1st Mississippi Cavalry, Corps Frederique,
    86
1st South Carolina Volunteer Regiment,
    71–72, 88, 118
1st Tennessee Heavy Artillery, 73, 86
1st United States Colored Cavalry, 75
Fleming, Walter L., 23, 25, 28, 29
    perception of, on African American
        court officials, 26–27
Florida
    African Americans as military police
        in, 102
    liberation of slaves in, 71
    scouting for Union army in, 130
Forgery, spies engaged in, 140–141
Fort Duana, South Carolina, 87
Fortier, Michael, 14, 17n20
    as major for battalion of free blacks,
        8, 11

Fort Mims, African American militia
    defense of, 2–3
Fort Monroe, confinement of Butler,
    Benjamin at, 149
Fortress Monroe
    escape of slaves to, 42
    location of rebels near, 149
    move of Mrs. Jefferson Davis from, 137
Foster, J. G., 92
Fourteenth Amendment, 53
4th United States Colored Heavy Artillery,
    75
Freedman's Bureau
    African Americans in Chattanooga and,
        115
    Campbell, Tunis as agent of, 116–117
    control of black court and, 115
    formation of, 54
Freedmen
    privileges of serving in the American
        army, 110
    settlement in Mitchelville, 111
FreeMen of Color, 6
Fremont, John C., 46–47
    on employment of African Americans in
        the Union army, 121
    on liberation of slaves and, 43, 48–49,
        56
    value of slave labor and, 44
French law, liberation of slaves and, 55
*From the Virginia Plantation to the National
    Capital* (Langston), 34
Fugitive slaves, protection of, 46

Gallus, Uncle, 126
Garrett, S. S., 83, 84
Garrison, William Lloyd, 35
    Tubman, Harriet and, 132
Gayarre, Charles, 7, 13, 17n10
Gendarmerie, 11
Genes, Jno A., 91
Georgia. *See also* Savannah, Georgia
    liberation of slaves in, 71
    scouting for Union army in, 130
Gillisonville, South Carolina, 87
Gillmore, Quincy A., information given
    to, 129
Glover, William, 35

Grahamville, South Carolina, 87
Grant, Ulysses S., 138
  on Africans as social slaves, 55–56
Greenleaf, Simon, 37
Gregory, Salomon, as scout assistant to
    Tubman, Harriet, 132
Guerilla warfare, 81
Gurley, spying on, 126

Hall, Prince, 38
Halleck, W. Henry, 46–47
  convictions of, on slaves, 46–47
  expulsion of African Americans at
    Union lines, 52–53
  on liberation of African slaves, 46
  opposition of entrance of African
    Americans into Union lines, 47
Hallowell, E. N., 93
  brutal nature of, 92
  prison camp under, at Morris Island,
    94–98
Hammock, South Carolina, 87
Hampton, Virginia
  African Americans in, 116
  provision of information in seizing, 129
Hastings, Russell, 83, 84
Haynes, Lorenzo, 86
Hayward, Isaac, as scout assistant to
    Tubman, Harriet, 132
Headley, Phineas Camp, 78
Heer, Barttholomew Van, 77
Helena, Arkansas, 101
Hewett, James R., 91
Hewett, Janet B., 64, 65, 75, 78, 86
Higginson, Thomas Wentworth, 77, 78,
    79, 80, 82
  on employment of African Americans in
    the army, 121
  formation of black regiment by, 71–72,
    131
  on need for arming blacks, 110
  on value of Tubman, Harriet, 132
Hilton Head, South Carolina
  African Americans stationed at, 85
  contraband in, 111
  Hunter, David's command at, 44
  9th United States Colored Infantry at, 86
  Union occupation of, 129–130

Hinds, Thomas, 3
Historical Collection of Ohio (Howe), 34
History of New Hampshire (Belknap), 31
Hoffman, William, 63
Hooker, Joseph, discovery of Dabney after
    escape, 147–148
Houston, Hubert Todd, 142
Howard, William D. M., 35
Howe, Henry, 34
Hoyt, Henry, 86
Human intelligence, as instrument of the
    Civil War, 120
Hunter, David, 79
  carrying of arms by black men under
    the command of, 70
  disbanding of regiment of, 72
  emancipation of slaves and, 43, 48
  employment of Tubman by, 131
  enlistment of African Americans, 70
  formation of military regiment of
    people of African descent, 44
  formation of the Louisiana Native
    Guard by, 72
  on formation of unofficial regiments of
    people of color, 48–49
  support of War Department to organize
    African American regiments,
    70–71
  on use of African Americans for
    Confederate controlled
    fortifications, 120
  value of slave labor and, 44
Hurd, John Codman, 14–15
Hurricane Plantation, 22
  administration of criminal justice on,
    23, 24
  African American law enforcement
    officers at, 22–23
  management of slaves at, 142
  Montgomery, Benjamin, as manager of,
    142, 143
  Montgomery, Benjamin's plan to protect
    Davis' property, 144–146
  purchase of, by Montgomery plantation,
    145

Illinois, black codes in, 34
Indiana, black codes in, 34

The Inner Life of Abraham Lincoln: Six Months at the White House (Carpenter), 50
Instructions for the Government of Armies of the United States in the Field, 67
Iraq War, 75
Irish police, 84
   black soldiers and, 84
Island No. 63, Mississippi, 101

Jackson, Andrew, service of African Americans in militia in War of 1812, xiv, 2, 15–16
Jem
   employment in US Secret Service, 124
   as helpful in guiding Pinkerton, Allen, in Memphis, 123–124
Jennison, Charles, 45
   dislike for slavery, 44
   value of slave labor and, 44
Johnson, Andrew, veto of, over Freedmen's Bureau, 54
Johnston, Edward Austin, 22, 141
Jones, E., appointment as special police commissioner, 11
Jones, James H.
   as body servant of Davis, Jefferson, 140–146
   Confederate missions entrusted with, 140
   employment by Davis, Jefferson, as servant, 136–137
   loyalty of, 141, 145–146
   mental and intellectual capacities of, 141
   during Reconstruction, 141–142
Jurymen, African Americans as, 25–26

Kanon, Tom, 2
Kansas black regiment, formation of, 71
Kastor, Peter J., 10, 12
Keating, John McLeod, 84
Kerr, Lewis, as major for battalion of free blacks, 8, 11
King, Edward, 118
King, Grace Elizabeth, 6
King, Susie Taylor, visit to St. Simon's Island, 118
Kingsley, Z, slaves of, 21

Knoxville, Tennessee, as center of railroad communications, 99

Ladies Island, enlistment of African Americans in, 71
Lambkin, Prince, duties of, 80
Langston, John Mercer, 34, 35, 73
   as city councilman in Oberlin, Ohio, 34
   election to the Board of Education, 34
   law enforcement duties of, xvi
Lapp, Rudolph M., 35
Latour, Arsene Lacarriere, 19n41
Law enforcement
   African Americans in, 75–80
   before the Civil War in the Northern States, 31–39
   inLouisiana, 1, 4–16, 102
   in Louisiana, 4–16
   as militiamen pre Civil War in Tennessee and Mississippi territory, 1–4
   duties in, during the Civil War, 62–102
   emergency services as, 87–88
   law and order in Civil War settlements and villages, 110–118
   maintenance of law and order in the plantations before the Civil War, 20–29
   patroling as valued, 80–87
   spies, scouts and informants and, 120–134, 136–139, 147–149
The Law of Freedom and Bondage (Hurd), 14–15
Law of Nations, 67–68. *See also* Constitution of the United States
   executive of war and maintenace of peace under the, 69
   liberation of slaves and, 55
   protection of African Americans by, 43
   protection of prisoners of war by, 91, 92
Lawson, James, provision of scouting information by, 128–131
Lawton, Hattie, secret operative mission of, 126
Leidesdorff, William Alexander, 35
Leonards Town, African Americans in, 126
Lewis, Frank, emancipation of, 43

Lewis, Pryce, Pinkerton, Allen, on
    performance of, 127
Liberty Party, 34
Lieber, Francis, 67, 92
Lincoln, Abraham, 136
    adjudication of cases and, 92
    appeasing strategy of, 47
    call for volunteers from African Americans
        on enlistment into army, 53
    Confederate hope for assassination of,
        122
    efforts to appease Confederate states
        officials, 43
    emancipation proclamation as military
        necessity, 56
    first Emancipation Proclamation of,
        49–50
    on freeing of slaves, 45–46
    friendship with Pinkerton, Allen, 125
    inauguration speech of, 45
    internationalization of Civil War by, 67
    introduction of Douglass, Frederick
        to, 74
    lack of acknowledgement of seceded
        states, 67
    nullifaction of Fremont's proclamation
        on liberation of African Americans,
        43, 44
    on preservation of Union as sole reason
        for Civil War, 47
    protection of Brierfield and Hurricane
        Estates and, 144
    on purpose of Civil War, 45, 71
    revoke of Hunter's decision to organize
        regiment of runaway slaves, 71
    second Emancipation Proclamation of,
        51
    on Seward's advice on postponing
        liberation of slaves, 50
    support for Trumbull's proclamation
        and, 46
Lincoln and the Negro (Porter and Quarles),
    62
Little Rock, Arkansas, 60th United States
    cColored Infantry at, 90, 93
Livandais, Jacques Enould, appointment as
    special police commissioner, 11
Lloyd, Edward, 21

Locklier, Jeffrey, as free African American
    militiamen in War of 1812, 2
Lorenzo, Thomas, formation of regiments
    of people of color and, 54
Lossing, Benson John, 149
Lothrop, T. K., 38
Louisiana. See also Natchitoches,
    Louisiana; New Orleans; Port
    Hudson, Louisiana
    African Americans in, 82
        arming of, 8
        in law enforcement, xv, 1, 4–16, 102
        with patrol services, 10, 81
        in policing, 82
    Claiborne, William C. C., as governor
        in, 4–5
    statehood for, 13–14
    transfer from French to the
        Americans, 6
    white native dislike for black people in,
        5–6
Louisiana Native Guard, 82
    formation of, 72
Louisiana Purchase, employment of
    African Americans in militia
    during era of, 5
Lovett, Bobby, 2
Lucas, William D., 115
Lussat, Pierre Clement de, 5
Lyon, Nathaniel, freeing of slaves by, 44

Maccon, Allen, law enforcement duties
    of, xvi
Madison, James
    concerns over safety of New Orleans, 8
    as Secretary of State, 10
Magaw, Samuel, provision of information
    to, 128
Magruder, John, preparation to seize
    Newport and Hampton, 129
Mallory, Charles, slaves of, 42
Mallory, Stephen, as Confederate Secretary
    of Navy, 67
Malloy, Adam Gale, 68
Manning, Van, 96
Martin, Francois-Xavier
Maryland, recruitment of black regiments
    in, 72–73

McClellan, George B., as commander in chief of the Union Army, 125
McDonough, John, slaves of, 21, 22
Mckaye, James, 47–48
Mcphersonville, South Carolina, 87
Memminger, Christopher, as Confederate Secretary of the Treasury, 67
Memphis, Tennessee
    establishment of Camp Pickering near, 84
    railroads in, 101
    riots of 1866 in, 83, 84
    Union control of, 96
Memphis Charleston Railroad, guarding of bridges on, 101
Men of color. See African Americans
    as volunteer-citizen soldiers, 70
Mexican War, 28
Michel, Constant, service in law enforcement by, 9
Military police, history of, 76–77
Mississippi. See also Vicksburg, Mississippi
    African Americans in, xvi, 82
        as military police in, 82, 102
        in militia, 2–4
        in patrol services, 81
    Claiborne, William C. C., as governor in, 4–5
Missouri
    guerilla burning of railroad bridges in, 127–128
    recruitment of black regiments in, 72–73
Mitailleuse Regua gun, 95
Mitchel, Ormsby M., 111, 112
    formation of African American regiments and, 121
Mitchelville, South Carolina, 110, 111–114
    governing of, 112–113
    school attendance in, 114
Money laundering, spies engaged in, 140–141
Montgomery, Alabama, as first capital of the Confederate States, 136
Montgomery, Benjamin
    Davis, Jefferson's recoup of property from, 144–146

emancipation of, 144
loyalty of, to Davis family, 145–146
as manager of Hurricane plantation, 142, 143
plan of, to preserve Hurricane plantation from Union soldiers, 142–144
sale of Davis properties to, 145
services to Davis, Jefferson, and Davis, Joe, 141–146
Montgomery, Isaiah
    building of Mount Bayou, 145
    legacy of, 145
    as Mississippi convention delegate for amending the Constitution, 145
Montgomery, James, 73
    on employment of African Americans in the Union army, 121
    as mission commander, 131
    Tubman as spy and guide under, 132
Moore, Frank, 148
Moore, Thomas Overton, formation of Louisiana Native Guard and, 72
Moore (slave), on importance of fighting for the cause of the Union, 47–48
More, Frank, 147
Morganza, Louisiana, 85
Morris, Robert, 37–38
Morris Island, South Carolina, Union prison camp, 64–65
    under Colonel Hallowell at, 94–98
    duties of the guards at, 97–98
    management of prisoners at, 92
    regulations in, 95–97
    Waggoner Camp at, 94
Mount Bayou, 23, 145
Murray, John Ogden, 64, 65, 91, 92, 93–94, 96–97

Nashville, Tennessee
    African Americans in, 81
        law enforcement duties of, 81, 102
    Confederate spirit in, 76
    defense of railroads in, 99
    River Cumberland as essential to, 100–101
Nashville and Chattanooga Railroad, 99
Nashville and Northwestern Railroad, 100

Natchitoches, Louisiana
  formation of police corps of free blacks
    in, 15
  maintenance of peace in the parish of,
    14
Naval History of the Civil War (Porter), 130
The Negro in the American Revolution
    (Porter and Quarles), 62
The Negro in the Civil War (Porter and
    Quarles), 62
Nell, William Cooper, 37
New England, town system in colonies
    in, 20
New England Historical Genealogy (1885),
    32
New England Historical Genealogy Society,
    31
*New Hampshire Annual Register and the
    United States Calendar*, 32
Newmarket, New Hampshire
  Cheswell, Wentworth, as justice of peace
    in, xv
  law enforcement in, 31
New Orleans. *See also* Louisiana
  Bore, Etienne de, as mayor of, 11
  Claiborne's concerns over security of, 8
  establishment of City Guard in, 12–13
  fall of, in Civil War, 143
  guarding of General Hospital at, 101
  military duties of Butler in, 149
  relationships of free African Americans
    with Claiborne, William C. C.
    in, 5
New Orleans, Battle of (1814)
  African American drummers in, 9
  free men of color in, 10
  militia in, 9, 16
Newport, provision of information in
    seizing, 129
New York, boroughs in, 20
9th United States Colored Infantry, 75,
    85, 86
Noble, Jordan, service as drummer during
    Battle of New Orleans, 9
Norfolk, Virginia, 93
North Carolina, parishes in, 20
North Edisto, African Americans in,
    117–118

Oak Point Plantation in Beaufort, 79
Oberholtzer, Ellis Paxson, 62, 82
Old Van Lew Mansion, 137
O'Neal, Charles, lost of life during patrol
    duties, 118
Ossabow, Campbell, Tunis's rule of, 117
Overseer, plantation, 27–28

Palfrey, John, 37
Pardon, Davis, Jefferson's power to, 27
Parker, Arthur, 140
Parton, James, 149
  liberation of slaves and, 55
Patroling, 80–87
Patton, James, on Butler, Benjamin,
    115–116
Pemberton, James
  Davis, Jefferson employment of, 28–29,
    136–137
  as plantation judge at Brierfield
    Plantation, 25, 142
Pennsylvania, boroughs in, 20
People of color. *See also* African Americans;
    slaves
  enlistment of, into Union army, 52
  formation of unofficial regiments
    of, 48
  permission from war department of
    formation of regiment of, 53
  Stevens, Thaddeus' interest in cause of,
    52–53
Petersburg, Virginia, combat operations
    in, 63
Phelps, John W.
  on employment of African Americans in
    the Union army, 121
  on employment of African slaves, 47
  on formation of unofficial regiments of
    people of color, 48
  value of slave labor and, 44
Philipps, Ulrich Bonnell, 22
Phillips, Wendell, 35
  Tubman, Harriet and, 132
Pierce, E. I., 117
Pierce, Edward L., 71
Pierce, L. Thomas, 100
Piernas, Pedro, 5
Piloting of ships, 80

Pinkerton, Allen
    friendship with Lincoln, Abraham, 125
    Jem as helpful in guiding, in Memphis,
        123–124
    management of the US Secret Service
        and, 122, 125
    observation of spying and scouting by,
        121
    on Scobell, John, as spy and scout, 122,
        124–127
    screening of contrabands for
        information, 123
    Underground Railroad and, 125
Pinkerton National Detective Agency, 125
Plantations. See also Brierfield plantation;
        Hurricane Plantation
    African Americans as officers of court, 25
    maintenance of law and order in pre-
        civil war, 20–29
    self-governing approach in, 23
Pocahontas, Tennessee, 101
Pocotoligo, South Carolina, 26th US
        Infantry stationing at, 87
Poindexter, Ellidgea, 39
Point Coupee Parish, black militia in,
        9–10
Point Lookout, Maryland, 96
    prisoners-of-war in, 63–64
    white soldiers as guards over prisoners of
        war at, 93
Polk, James, 35
Pomeroy, Samuel
    on emancipation of slaves, 52
    on eqal pay to military men, 74
Porter, Andrew, 125
    law enforcement duties of, 77
Porter, David Dixon, 62, 80, 85, 130
Port Hudson, Louisiana, 101
    Convalescent Camp at, 102
Port Royal, Saxton as commander of, 100
Price, Isaiah, 111
Prince, Caesar, as free African American
        militiamen in War of 1812, 2
Prisoners-of-war
    blacks as Confederate, 74
    exchange process for, 75
    guarding, 62–63, 90–94
    in point Lookout, Maryland, 63–64

Provost marshal, law enforcement and
        judiciary duties of, 76–77

Quarles, Benjamin, 62, 78

Railroad, control of, 99, 100
Railroad bridges
    guarding of, 101
    guerilla burning of, in Missouri,
        127–128
Railroads. See under Underground
        Railroad
Ramsdell, William, 98
Rawland, Dunbar, 101
Reagan, John H., as Confederate
        Postmaster General, 67
Reconstruction
    Jones, James H., during, 141–142
    Smalls, Robert, during, 133
Reed, Iram, emancipation of, 43
Refugees, treatment of escaped, 69
Reid, Whitelaw, 78
    Mitchelville and, 111–112
Reilly, Robinson, 5
Renfro, Robert, as free African American
        militiamen in War of 1812, 2
Revolutionary War
    body servants for generals in, 76
    military police activities in, 77–78
    provost marshals in, 76–77
Richmond, Virginia
    African American spies in the
        Confederate White House in,
        136–139
    as capital of the Confederate States, 136
    as center for hope in assassination of
        Lincoln, 122
    combat operations in, 63
    construction of fortification around,
        126
    fall of, 88, 141
    move of Davis, Jefferson, to, 136–137,
        140, 143
Rightor, Henry, 10, 11–12
Ripley, James W., 133
Rivers, Prince, 79–80, 82
Roberts, Robert, 38
Roberts, Sarah C., 38

Robertsville, South Carolina, 87
Rock, John Sweet, 38
The Roster of Union Soldiers, 1861-1865
    (Hewett), 75
Runaway slaves
    Butler's welcoming of, 120
    employment as spies, 123

St. Catherine's Island, African Americans
    in, 117
St. Mary's River, piloting of ship on, 80
St. Simon's Island, black watchmen in,
    117–118
Saint Helena Island, enlistment of African
    Americans in, 71
Sarah C. Roberts v. *The City of Boston*, 38
Savannah, Georgia
    formation of coastal government in,
        116
    information from runaway slaves on,
        129
    move of Mrs. Jefferson Davis to, 137
    scouting information on, 129
Saxton, Rufus, 70, 100
    as architect of social programs to assist
        freed African Americans, 116
    on formation of unofficial regiments of
        people of color, 48
Schaff, Morris, 25, 27, 28, 142
Schofield, John M.
    African American collecton of
        information for, 127–129
    removal of, 88–89
Scobell, John
    employment by Union, 125–126
    intellectual ability of, 123
    Pinkerton, Allen, on performance of,
        126–127
    as spy, 122, 123–124
Scott, George
    provision of scouting information by,
        128–129
    as Union spy, 149
2nd Wisconsin Infantry, 63
Second Confiscation and Militia Act (July
    17, 1862), 48
Self-governing approach, in plantation
    government, 21, 23

17th United States Colored Infantry, 76
74th United States Colored Infantry, 82,
    93
Seward, William
    perception on liberation of slaves and,
        50–51
    on value of Tubman, Harriet, 132
Sharpe, George H., as chief of the Bureau
    of Military Information, 138
Shaw, Francis George, 73
    on employment of African Americans in
        the Union army, 121
Shaw, Robert Gould
    as commander of 54th regiment of the
        Massachusetts Volunteer Infantry,
        73
    death of, as Fort Wagner, 73
Sheriffs
    selection of slaves as, 23–24
    title of, as antiquated, 24–25
Ship Island, Mississippi, 91
Silters, Sandy, as scout assistant to
    Tubman, Harriet, 132
Simon's Island, African American soldiers
    in, 71
16th Infantry Regiment, 77
60th United States Colored Infantry, 90
62nd United States Colored Infantry,
    85–86, 90
Slave disorders, quelling of, by African
    American militia, 5
Slaves. *See also* African Americans; Escaped
    slaves; Runaway slaves
    admission into Union lines, 43–44
    civil rights protection for, 43, 54
    crimes by, 21
    dependence on federal government
        during Civil War, 118
    emancipation of, in rebel states, 54–55
    employment in corrections, 26
    escape to Fortress Monroe, 42
    freeing of, 42, 43–44
    identification of, as contraband, 43
    keeping fugitive, in the Union lines, 42
    liberation of, as psychological weapon to
        demoralize their masters, 44
    military enlistment of, 42
    as property of white men, 111

Slaves (*continued*)
    protection from the U.S. government,
        42
    protection of fugitive, 46
    return to masters and, 46
    selection of, as sheriffs and constables,
        23–24
    self-governing approach to, 21
    social, 55–56
    value of labor, 44
Smalls, Robert
    as commander of *USS Planter*, 80, 130,
        133
    employment as pilot by Union officials,
        130
    information provided to Union by, 130,
        133–134
Smith, Gerrit, on value of Tubman,
    Harriet, 132
Smith, Samuel, defense of Fort Mims by,
    2–3
Snead, Thomas L., emancipation of slaves
    of, 43
Social slaves, 55–56
Sopelo, Campbell, Tunis's rule of, 117
South Carolina. *See also* Beaufort, South
    Carolina; Charleston, South
    Carolina; Walterborough, South
    Carolina
    African American population in, 82
    black soldier policing in, 82
    empowerment of black soldiers with
        patrol services in, 81
    liberation of slaves in, 71
    parishes in, 20
    scouting for Union army in, 130
    Taylor, Susie King, as scout and nurse in
        Native Guard in, 131
Southern states, secession of, 136, 137
Spaulding, David, 98
Spencer (free black), work of, in
    Richmond, 138–139
Stanton, Edwin McMasters, 72, 100
    on importance of African American
        assistance, 120–121
    introduction of Douglass, Frederick
        to, 74
    on pay of the black soldiers, 74

Stevens, Isaac I., 70
Stevens, Thaddeus, advocation of
    enlistment of people of color, 52
Still, William, 36
Stoneman, George, 83
Stuart, Henry Middleton, 79
Sumner, Charles, 37, 45
    on eqal pay to military men, 74
    Tubman, Harriet and, 132
Supplement to the Official Records of the
    Union and Confederate Armies, 96

Tatnell, Isaac
    information provided to Union army
        by, 129
    as source of information for Union
        army, 129
Taylor, Susie King, 70, 74, 87–88
    as scout and nurse in the South Carolina
        Native Guard, 131
10th United States Colored Infantry, 75
Tennessee. *See also* Memphis, Tennessee;
    Nashville, Tennessee
    African American contributions in, xvi
    African American enrollment in militia
        in, 1–4
    recruitment of black regiments in,
        72–73
    white soldiers enforcement of law in, 79
Ten person rule, 96
3rd Massachusetts regiment, 127
3rd United States Cavalry, 75
3rd United States Colored Artillery, 83,
    86, 87
13th Regiment, 73
Thirteenth Amendment, 37, 56
31st United States Colored Troops, 90
36th Battalion, Virginia Confederate
    Army, 143
36th U.S. Colored Infantry, 63
33rd United States Colored Infantry
    Regiment, 30. *See also* 1st South
    Carolina Volunteers
Thomas, Lorenzo, 72–73
    recruitment of people of color regiment,
        54–55
Thomas, Phillip, as free African American
    militiamen in War of 1812, 2

Thomas, Pierre, 5
Thompson, Clara Mildred, 116
Toombs, Robert, as Confederate Secretary
    of State, 67
Trenholm, George A., 89
Trial by jury, 23
A Tribute for the Negro (Armistead), 37
Trowbridge, Charles, 71
    on formation of unofficial regiments of
        people of color, 48
Trowbridge, John Towsend, 78, 99, 115
Trumbull, Hon., on establishment of
    Freedmen's Bureau, 54
Trumbull, Lyman, freedom for slaves on
    entrance into Union lines, 46
Tubman, Harriet
    as part of the Underground Railroad,
        131–133
    as spy, scout, and nurse, 122, 130–133
Turner, Uncle, 126
12th Regiment Infantry, 73
    role of, in defense of railroad in
        Nashville, xiv*n*2
26th United States Colored Infantry, 87
Twilight, Alexander Lucius
    election to House of Representatives, 35
    as teacher, 36
Tybee Island, scouting information on,
    129

Underground Railroad
    Pinkerton, Allen, and, 125
    Tubman, Harriet, as part of, 131–133
The Underground Railroad (Still), 36
Union
    destruction of property held by slave
        owners in, 142
    escaped slaves as assets of, 120
    freedom of slaves on entrance into, 46
    role of military police, in success of war,
        75
United States Navy
    African American runaway slaves as
        pilots in, 129
    benefit from African American
        informants and spies, 123
United States Secret Service
    employment of Jem in, 124

jobs engaged in, 140–141
Pinkerton, Allan, management of, 122,
    125
USS Planter, Smalls as commander of, 80,
    130, 133

Van Lew, Elizabeth, employment of
    Bowser, Mary Elizabeth by,
    137–139
Vashon, George B., 38–39
Velder, O. F., 84
Vellio, Joseph, 3
Vicksburg, Mississippi, 84–85
    fall of, 85
    occupation of, 89
Victoria, Texas, African American soldier
    control of city jail in, 98
Virginia. *See also* Richmond, Virginia
    under constitutional law, 68
    liberation of slaves in, 68
    parishes in, 20

Waggoner Camp (Morris Island), 94
Walker, LeRoy Pope, as Confederate
    Secretary of War, 67
Walterborough, South Carolina, 87
War between the States. *See* Civil War
War of 1812, 74
    African Americans in militia in, xiii, xiv,
        2, 16
War of Northern Agression. *See* Civil War
War of Secession. *See* Civil War
War of the Rebellion. *See* Civil War
*The War of the Rebellion: A Compliation of
    the Official Records of the Union and
    Confederate Armies*, 65
Washburn, Emory, 37
Washington, Booker T., 22, 145
Washington, George, security of, 76
Watmough, Penrod, Tatnall's service to,
    129
Watson, Thomas Edward, 64, 65, 92
Watson's Magazine, 65
Webster, Laura Joseph, 71
Webster, Timothy
    Pinkerton, Allen, on performance of,
        127
    spying and, 126

Weil, Francois, 10, 12
Wentworth, Thomas
    on formation of unofficial regiments of
        people of color, 48
    Tubman as spy and guide under, 132
Western and Atlantic Railroad, 99
Whipple, Prince, 76
Whipple, William, 76
Whittier, John G., 35
Wiley, Edgar Jolls, 35–36
Wilkinson, James, 11
    recognition of existing black militia, 8
William (Negro), as waiter in Mississippi
        Militia, 3
Williams, James, 71
Wilson, Charles, freedom of slaves in
        Washington and, 51

Wilson, Henry, 45
    on equal pay to military men, 74
    on southern preparation for war, 72
Wilson, James, on amending Iowa
        Constitution on abolition of
        slavery, 56
Wilson, Joseph Thomas, 2, 91
Wintrop, Scott, 149
    provision of information to, 129
Woodland, Isaac
    appointment as grain inspector, 36–37
    as runaway slave, 36
Wool, John E., pay for contraband owned
        by, 42
Woolfolk, Austin, 21

Yates, Henry, Jr., 87

ABOUT THE AUTHOR

LIEVIN KAMBAMBA MBOMA is an independent researcher with a focus in law enforcement during peace and war time. He holds a B.S. in criminal justice from Tennessee State University and received his master's degree in criminal justice from Tennessee State University and Middle Tennessee State University. He is a winner of the National Conference of Christian and Jews "Brotherhood/Sisterhood Award" and was also a nominee for the Mary Catherine Strobel "Volunteer of the Year Award." He is the author of the book *African Descendants in Colonial America: Impact on the Preservation of Peace, Security, and Safety in New England, 1638-1783* (forthcoming book).

Currently, he is working on two book manuscripts titled: *African American Lawmen, 1867-1877 Vol.1* and *African American Lawmen, 1877-1920, Vol.2*. He also has an unpublished manuscript titled *Customary Law Enforcement in the Democratic Republic of the Congo (Kingdoms and Empires)*. In addition to these works, Mboma has collected pertinent data on the inclusion of African descendants in the security apparatus of the Southern colonies (Virginia, North Carolina, South Carolina, and Maryland) during colonial wars.

CPSIA information can be obtained
at www.ICGtesting.com
Printed in the USA
LVHW09*0224030918
588983LV00004B/9/P